PAUL XXX

The Sickletree Hours

Paul Dibbens

A COLLECTION OF SHORT STORIES THAT EXPLORE THE THEMES OF LOVE, HEALING AND TIME

Illustrated by Tim Porter

Please direct all enquiries to the author:
Ivy Lodge, Green Lane
Shipston on Stour, Warwickshire CV36 4HG
paul@mustardhot.com
www.pauldibbens.com

ISBN: 978-1-80068-249-8

Designed and typeset in Sabon 11/16pt by Mustard Design
Printed in the United Kingdom

For the tribe

Finding Sickletree

THE TOWN OF SICKLETREE can be an awkward place to find and that's the way we'd like it to stay, hence the change of name to protect the innocent. Many have spent their lives scouring the length of the valley of the tranquil River Windrush that runs throughout England's beautiful Cotswolds to try and uncover our Shangri-La and not found it. Call us Nimbys, no matter — but we believe the fewer people that discover its hidden charms the better. In fact, most of the country doesn't know that the town actually exists outside of dreams but I can assure you it does, having wandered unintentionally into its embrace some forty-odd years ago and having never felt the urge to leave. Back in the day there were towns like Sickletree all over England, tucked away in hidden places and filled with inhabitants who were content to embrace the old ways and sleepwalk through their lives, but now such places are as rare as teeth on a hen.

Where you might still find this island of serenity in a sea of green, however, is in the place you sometimes visit when your mind is wandering just before sleep. There you can walk its darkened streets under a star-dusted, raven-black sky (no street lights after twelve), trace the sleepy river where it wraps a silvered arm around the town and throw a polished brown stone back into the water to help it resume its eternal journey to the sea. Or maybe take a drink in one of its pubs if you are allowed a lock-in (there's no police after dark so why not?). On a Saturday morning you can wander into the Market Square for a paper and maybe glimpse my father-in-law's ghost, leaning against his bike outside of the fish shop and holding court about all things country and the rest. Here, in the busy crowd, most will smile and wish you a good morning and even if they pass you by in silence, wrapped up in their own worlds, you will feel no malice. It's a gentle place. And when you rise you will know you've spent the night in Sickletree as you'll have slept like a log and awoken to the smell of woodsmoke and the tinkle of frosted milk bottles on your doorstep.

For people who value their privacy and security from the outside world above anything else, Sickletreans are the kindest and least frantic of people. Even when engaged in business and commerce there's always time to stop and ask how things are with your life and how your day is going. They are accepting and true to each other, supportive and calm and full of quiet resolve and humour. Maybe the tranquility of their home fosters such qualities, who knows? Sickletree skies are vast and calm, its fruitful fields are sheltered havens from the tempests of the coast and its trees are tall and ancient and guard the town like immovable sentinels.

But when all is said and done you needn't think that even if you find our town that you'll necessarily be immediately accepted. It takes years to be granted your Sickletree passport and sometimes the powers-that-be still refuse citizenship to the loud, brash and boastful that wander in from the cities and try and take over. Whatever! Before you drift off to sleep, give thanks that in this increasingly challenging world such people and places still exist and our hidden gem remains a secret that only a lucky few know where to find.

Sickletree — your secret is safe with me.

Paul Dibbens
February 2022

A Lifetime in a Day

A BOOK OF HOURS was a devotional prayer book that was popular in Europe in the Middle Ages and is the most common type of medieval illuminated manuscript that survives in the modern world. Almost all of them contain a similar collection of texts, prayers and psalms that were used as aids for Christian devotion. Each Book of Hours is unique and they were the best sellers of their day.

Although artwork is minimal in many of the books and usually restricted to the illumination of initial letters, examples that were created for wealthier patrons were often intricately decorated. "Painted prayers" in the form of picturesque scenes of rural life combined with sacred images were recurring motifs used to enhance the pages.

Books of Hours were usually written in Latin (the Latin name for them is *horae*), although there are many entirely or partially written in vernacular European languages, especially Dutch and French. The English term "primer" is usually now reserved for those books written in English.

Thousands of Books of Hours have survived to the present day and continue to inspire the world with their beauty, craftsmanship and piety. Perhaps the most famous of these is the *Très Riches Heures du Duc de Berry*. After three centuries in obscurity, the *Très Riches Heures* began to gain wide recognition in the late nineteenth century, despite having only limited exposure at the Musée Condé just outside of Paris. Its miniatures helped to shape an idealised image of the Middle Ages in the collective imagination.

This is particularly true for the calendar images which offer vivid portrayals of peasants performing seasonal agricultural tasks as well as aristocrats set in ceremonial situations against backdrops of imposing medieval architecture. A lot of these buildings are the properties of the book's patron, John, Duke of Berry. They truly are windows to another world.

A typical Book of Hours is an abbreviated form of the breviary, a liturgical book used for marking the Divine Office which is a collection of prayers, psalms, readings and hymns that are recited at stated hours of the day. These Canonical Hours, as they are called, are still used in sequestered religious institutions to form the basis of daily worship in monastic life.

So, if the Canonical Hours are used to structure a day, then perhaps they can also illustrate the different phases of a lifetime.

MATINS (SMALL HOURS) / THE CHILD
LAUDS (DAWN) / THE ADOLESCENT
PRIME (EARLY MORNING) / THE YOUNG MAN
TERCE (MID MORNING) / THE ADULT
SEXT (MIDDAY) / MATURITY
NONES (MID AFTERNOON) / OLD AGE
VESPERS (EVENING) / DECLINE
COMPLINE (NIGHT) / EXTINCTION

The Sickletree Hours explores the themes of love, healing and time based on personal experience. The stories have been illuminated with a few careful brush strokes of imagination and were written with a knowledge and appreciation of calmer and more meditative people and times.

Paul Dibbens
February 2022

THE TREE OF LIFE IS GROWING
WHERE THE SPIRIT NEVER DIES
AND THE BRIGHT LIGHT OF SALVATION
SHINES IN DARK AND EMPTY SKIES.

— BOB DYLAN —

Contents

I / MATINS

THE LATTER PART

OF VIGIL.

FROM 3AM

UNTIL DAWN.

THE CHILD

A Tortoise in the Kitchen

THE COUPLE WALKED THROUGH the cut in the chalk where the road sliced through the top of the downs as clean as a knife-wound to the bone. Below them a solitary road grey-snaked through the white valley and disappeared into a gap in the bank of frosted haze far away on the immense horizon. Drops of a dying sun's blood were caught in the trees and stained the forested hills that bracketed their destination. Many years later he was to regard this spot as the gateway to his home but for now the view, despite its forbidding bleakness, was as fresh to him as an uncut flower.

They'd had nothing to eat or drink since stopping at a golden-stoned church outside of Oxford in the middle of the day, where they had sat in the porch and shared a can of sickly orangeade and a frigid pastie that tasted like a newly-laid brick in cement. He had been grateful to avoid the noise of the thundering traffic for a brief period of stillness and shelter from the biting February northerly. She had been glad to get him off the road as he had seemed nervous and distracted. An unseen organist was practising his Bach which provided the perfect soundtrack to their meal: the performance finished abruptly with an echoed cough and a shuffle of papers followed by the sound of hurried footsteps on the stone-flagged floor and the slamming of a door.

Their long walk northwards into the wind began again, jacket collars raised around ears and heads bent to deflect the chill.

'Our noses are running and our feet smell. We must be built upside down,' he said, just to break the silence. She laughed, bless her, as she always did at his corny jokes.

They needed to reach their destination before nightfall as it wouldn't be safe to be walking this narrow, twisted road after dark. With every field they passed the white stuff drifted ever deeper as the strength of the wind stripped the fields bare of snow and trapped it in the secret hollows under the hedges and in the ridge and furrow ditches. Attempts at hitching went mostly unrewarded apart from a battered, pale-blue Triumph 2000, driven by a drunk who had trouble keeping his hands on the wheel and who became aggressive when they took a stand against his racist views.

Hours later and they were standing by the roadside on the top of the downs, shrouded in a diamond dust and looking out at the wonder of a pure Cotswold winter sunset that stretched before them off into Wales. Racing southwards was a threatening bank of cream-coloured cloud and before long the first flakes of its needle-snow struck them like a volley of arrows.

'How far?' he asked as he turned his back to the blow.

'Not sure,' she replied absently. 'Probably four or five miles?' She looked as if she could walk all night and wouldn't bother if she had to.

'It's magical, but scary,' said Danny as he studied the dramatic scene. 'I can't believe you used to live here. It's a hard landscape.'

'C.S. Lewis lived just down the road in Oxford. You are looking at the inspiration for Narnia.'

He looked at his watch. 3:50pm. The dying sun had already bled what little colour there had been from the day and a pallid twilight was around them. Headlight beams grew brighter with each passing vehicle and sporadically highlighted a blizzard that covered the road as quickly as drawing a blanket. Danny hadn't been this cold since the winter of 1962/3 when the sea had frozen fifty yards offshore and the drifts had lasted from Boxing Day night until the spring. That had been twelve years before.

'This wind's blowing straight from the Urinals.'

'I think you mean the Urals,' she said laughing

'That's what I said — the Urinals.'

'You daft bugger.'

'Lead on MacDuff,' he said. 'You know the way.'

***

The bedraggled and frozen couple walked hand-in-hand out of the night and past a short row of three-up, two-down council houses on the edge of town. They stood outside of the last house on the street at the place where the snow-blanketed countryside returned and stretched away into an illuminated night. The cloud had cleared and the star-flecked sky lit up the snowfields as if it were day. On the narrow concrete drive next to the back door of No 12 an ancient Morris Minor was parked in a drift, its tyres were flat and perished and its boot was open to the elements, revealing a ravaged leather tool bag and a well-worn Victorian pit pony saddle and harness. Inside the wreck were several bags of what appeared to be seed potatoes and a cat curled up on the driver's seat, cosy, smiling and dreaming of tins of sardines: how it was getting in and out was a mystery. Every window of the tiny house was lit with a tangerine radiance and from inside came the sound of a party.

They stood in the snow and listened to the clamour.

'Nervous?'

'Hmm.'

'Don't worry. You'll be alright. They don't bite.'

A window in the house opened and a single white plume of cigarette smoke escaped upwards into the night air.

'Looks like they've just elected a new Pope.'

'Oh, you won't find any Popes in there, believe me.'

'You sure? I did hear that Pius the Fourth likes a party.'

'He prefers discos.'

'I hope the party isn't for me.'

'Don't flatter yourself. This is just a normal Saturday evening.'

'Really?'

'Let's get it over with,' she said and tightened her grip on his gloveless hand.

***

There were no hugs, fuss or sickly shows of affection, just a quiet acceptance that Ellie and her new boyfriend had arrived. A clamour of kids ran into the kitchen and stared with audacious wonder at the couple as they stood on the mat and brushed the snow off each other's shoulders.

'Grannie Esther! Our Ellie's home.'

'Where've you been? All around the Wrekin?'

A tall man with a shock of dark hair and a drooping moustache tetchily asked the question. Despite the suffocating heat of the tiny kitchen he was wearing a heavy Aran sweater under a sheepskin coat. Danny immediately sensed a covert hostility.

'We hitched from Oxford and it took longer than we thought.'

Ellie filled a battered whistle-kettle from a screeching tap and put it on the Rayburn stove.

'Tea?' The tall man said nothing and just shook his head lightly in disdain and indicated his bottle of beer.

'This is Danny, by the way.' The tall man nodded once but remained silent and scanned the newcomer from head-to-toe with a dispassionate look instead.

At his feet was a straw-filled shoebox with, "I'm Slowcoach. Can you feed and water me every day please?" written on the lid. Inside, Danny caught a glimpse of a tortoise's shell.

Ellie went across the room, carefully parted the straw and peered inside as she gently rocked the box.

'I hope he's still alive,' she said, concerned.

'Don't ask me. How would I bloody know?' said the tall man. 'He's only a tortoise and they spend most of their lives asleep anyway, so what's the diff? Why don't you take its pulse if you're that worried?'

Ellie ignored him but Danny flinched at the outburst.

'If you need the loo it's out the back next to the chickens,' she said to Danny. 'There's no bathroom I'm afraid but the council say they're putting one in next spring. Mind you, they've been saying that for years.'

'Our Mother said to say your dinners are in the Rayburn,' the tall man added sulkily. He avoided looking at them as he said it.

Ellie persisted with the subject of animal welfare. 'Is Titmouse alright out on the Brickle in this? I hope she's got plenty of feed.'

'She's a Welsh pit pony. She's used to worse. If you're that worried get out there and feed her yourself. No? I didn't think so.'

'I'll go and check her after I've had something to eat.'

They sat in the kitchen and shared a bubbling bowl of rabbit stew that tasted strongly of sage and thyme. The children joined them at the table and watched them open-mouthed and with widened eyes that followed every spoonful from bowl to mouth.

The tall man casually leant back against the wall and chain-smoked in relays. He lit each cigarette from its fading ancestor and coolly studied the arrivals as would a magistrate before summing up and pronouncing sentence. The room was a dense fug of oven-heat, steam and second-hand smoke.

'From Portsmouth then? I went there once. Full of jumped-up cockney bullshitters.'

Danny politely put his hand over his mouth and finished chewing before speaking.

'Yep, that's where my family are from originally. London, I mean, not Pompey. They came out during the Blitz.' He ate and spoke quickly, being both starved and nervous. The intense cross-examination was putting him on edge.

'So, they did a runner when things got hot then.'

'Yes, well, it was a case of out of the frying pan —'

'Sounds like they were just plain frit in my book.'

'— into the fire,' persisted Danny. 'The bombing was almost as bad in Pompey.'

'They were just frit.'

'I think most people were. You'd be mad not to be.'

'Frit.'

Danny felt his hackles rise. What was this bloke's problem?

For now the tall man seemed satisfied with his work and ended the grilling with a shrug of his narrow shoulders before returning to silence. Danny felt dizzy as he usually did in moments of stress; the blood rushed to his head and his temples pounded. At the age of ten he had been coxing a galley in stormy seas with four angry oarsmen shouting and spitting at him and he had always given back as good as he got. Now he almost jumped at the sound of his own voice. Where had that brave boy gone?

'Ignore our Wayne,' said Ellie looking totally unconcerned by the exchange. 'He's like that with virtually everyone I bring home. Stick your plate in the sink and come on through to the house.'

She led him down a narrow corridor and into the chaos of the only other room on the ground floor.

The tall man gave their disappearing backs an acidic look but said nothing.

'Too much to drink and it's back to work Monday in the snow,' she whispered to Danny in the hall. 'He's okay when you get to know him, he just hates working in the cold.'

The noise and heat in the cramped front room was overpowering. How did they all fit in? There's not enough room in here to swing a cat, so no wonder the moggie's outside in the motor, thought Danny. Sensible creatures cats. Through a pounding partition wall, Led Zeppelin were busy battling a German oompah band who, in turn, were busy lifting the roof off the house next door. The blistering guitar riffs, supported by an enraged John Bonham and howling Robert Plant were overpowering the euphoniums and flugelhorns with ease. Another tall man, the double of the one in the kitchen, even down to the same moustache, turned up the volume to excruciating as he shouted to nobody in particular that, "Jimmy Page'll give Adolf Erlanger and his bunch of Nazis next door summat to think about". He then played air guitar to the gang of excitable kids who squealed with delight and joined in.

'That's our Laurie,' nodded Ellie in his direction. 'Him and Wayne are twins but they're as different as chalk and cheese.'

This was the part of the day that Danny had been dreading. He felt that he was the centre of attention of the throng when, in truth, most were too engrossed in a network of social interactions to take any notice of the newcomer. It was incredible how many bodies were packed into the room and the constant comings and goings made it seem like many more. He suddenly felt very hot and dizzy and put a hand on an ugly sideboard to steady himself as the emotional and physical exertions of the day caught up with him.

He hated being put on show but put on show he was. The pair circled the room as Ellie did the introductions.

'Ada, this is Danny.'

'Hello Ada.'

'What happened to Theo?' she asked indignantly.

'He was the last in a long line,' said a heavy set man next to her. He watched Danny for a reaction with an amused expression.

'This is Clifford, he's Ada's husband. And Theo wasn't my boyfriend, just a good mate.'

'A good mate? Well, that's a very interesting way of putting it,' said Clifford with a smirk.

'Ellie, where's Theo?' asked a small boy. 'I *liked* Theo — he always brought me sweets.' He stared at Danny accusingly.

'Peegee, you little monkey — you've got so *tall*,' exclaimed Ellie and she hugged the boy forcefully. 'Look at your dirty face. Have you been playing in the coal hole?'

A bottle of beer from one of the crates Danny had seen being cooled outside in a snowdrift was pressed into his hand. It was so cold he almost dropped it.

'*Mwah!*' A large brassy lady called Nora planted a smacker on his lips by way of greeting.

'Ooh, is this the new one? Everyone'll tell you I just *love* the men. Give us another quick. *Mwah!* Just one more. *Mwah!*'

Nora left him with an indelible crimson lipstick mark in the centre of his forehead that was to take two days to fade.

A tiny man who giggled and spoke non-stop gibberish was next in line. Just off the subs at Faslane was given as explanation.

'It'll take some time for him to settle down but he'll be fine in a week or two.'

'Danny, this is Moosher, our Wayne and Laurie's friend.'

'This is Gabriel, our Delilah's eldest boy.'

'This is Poppy, Laurie's wife.'

'You've met Peegee already.'

'Where's *Theo?*' said the small boy whiningly. 'And where's my *present?* Theo always brought me a present.'

'This is Rufus, our Bonnie's youngest.'

'And Fleur, her eldest.'

'Vincey —'

'Boxer —'

'My best friend, Tiny Pratt —'

'Meet the family, Rainbow —'

'Our Joy —'

'Ralph is our Bonnie's husband.'

'Peegee, go away and annoy somebody else, please —'

'Where's Theo?'

'I don't *know*, Sweetie.'

'I *liked* Theo.'

Sitting on a heap of cushions in a ragged chair and almost in the centre of a sweltering coal fire was the Queen Bee of the hive. Members of her brood buzzed everywhere, like a dense swarm of unsettled drones. This slim, birdlike woman in her mid-fifties, with the shrillest voice and piercing eyes, was bottle-feeding a huge baby on her lap: Danny hoped it wasn't hers but couldn't be sure — hopefully it was a grandchild.

She fired questions, observations and instructions at him as they came to mind. Once again he felt he was being tested but this time by a shrewd, highly intelligent and wise woman and he began to sweat. The conversation began politely enough.

'Is the snow deep on the roads?'

'I've seen nothing like it for years, Mrs Yeo.'

'Was your dinner okay, mister?'

'Lovely thanks. I've never had rabbit before.'

'Good. Have you had a beer?'

'Yes. Davenports Beer at Home? I don't think I've ever seen it in Pompey.'

'This heat makes me feel as giddy as a goat.' She fanned herself with the *Daily Mirror* and rocked the baby in the process.

'What's that bloody Dot Partridge doing in here? Anybody's welcome but her. She's a masterpiece having the nerve to show her face and no better than she should be.'

The conversation suddenly became more direct as she fixed him with a forceful stare. Then, out of the blue —

'Look after our Eleanor or else I'll set the twins on you.'

'Of course, Mrs Yeo,' he said alarmed.

'Only, you southerners can behave not very prettily at times.'

She smiled to herself, her power and influence over the young man had been indelibly confirmed.

'Only joking, but you know what I mean, mister?'

'Yes — at least I *think* I do.'

'Have you met my friend, Ada Tumbler?'

'I believe so,' he shouted above the din.

'We were in the Land Army together. We had some adventures, I can tell you.' She winked lasciviously. 'There was an Italian POW camp in the farm behind us. Lovely men. Kind, calm, gentle and helpful and they all looked like gods.'

The baby stopped feeding, burped, settled and immediately began snoring loud enough to be heard above the partying as the conversation changed direction again and became more intimate.

'Ellie says that you've had it tough growing up.'

He was surprised at the tears that came to his eyes and he just nodded and stared at the floor.

Yes, he'd had it tough for a very long time but it was hard to put into words so he studied the threadbare carpet with interest instead, hardly daring to lift his head in case of what she might say next.

'You've had a very difficult family life, our Eleanor said. You won't find it's the same with us.' This was said with a sudden and overwhelming kindness, compassion and acceptance.

'We've always done things differently here. Ah well, nothing can be done about it now, so best use it to make you stronger. Eh? We'll always tell you what we think. Are you okay with that?'

He nodded again but still didn't take his eyes off the floor. He didn't trust himself not to cry. It had been a long, trying day.

'Just remember. Don't get up to any of those pretty cockney tricks and you'll be fine in Sickletree, mister.' She winked at him.

'I'll do my best, I promise. And thanks for letting me stay.' Danny wasn't sure what cockney tricks she meant but he was sure that he didn't get up to them anyway.

'Now. That person sat over there that looks like Benny Hill is the Old Man. They call him Dimple. Go and have a chat with him and hopefully you won't get too bored. He sits in that chair like a lump of duff all day, stuffing his face and saying nothing to nobody unless it's about football, sprouts or horses. Then you can't shut him up.'

'Ah. It's a rare 'un outside tonight. 'Nuff ta friz ya ta d'yuth.'

Dimple may as well be speaking in a foreign language.

A plate, piled high with fried onions, mushrooms, tomatoes and an indeterminate grey mess was perched on his lap. On the side of his plate was a massive doorstop of bread which he would intermittently dunk into the gravy and then suck noisily. He was watching a rerun of the horse racing on a vintage black and white TV with the sound apparently down, though, in the surrounding cacophony, it was impossible to tell. His piercing blue eyes fixed Danny in calm contemplation as he chewed the cud in a bovine manner and he realised he was being sounded out once again.

'Enjoying your dinner, Mr Yeo?'

'Collared yud. Want some?'

If Danny had known what collared yud was he would have immediately left for home, straight back down that snowy road into the dark.

'See that wumman over theer with the gret big nubbers? Well, she got 'ers oojamacallits trapped in the mangle last weck. Well 'ers blouse and bra anyways, not 'ers wumman's bits. Oi sin it wiv me own oiyz and laffed 'til oi wuz fit t'ya bust.'

I think he's speaking Cotswold, guessed Danny. If I could only understand him I would probably get on with this man.

'Ha' you yutted yer rebbet stew?'

'I think so, Mr Yeo.' What was yutted?

Dimple suddenly became agitated and stared at the conclusion of a horse race on the TV whilst waving his knife up and down like a whip. 'Goowan, goowan,' he shouted. The room fell silent.

'Bugger! That ent roight. He's bin nobbled. Look, oi 'ad that 'un marked,' he said and showed Danny the paper where every horse in the race had a tick next to it.

'Unlucky, Mr Yeo.'

Dimple tutted, shook his head and for the first time since they had met looked as if life might have a little sadness in it after all.

'Grandad! Peegee pulled my hair,' shouted an excitable little girl with blond pigtails.

Dimple ignored her and started a new topic. The Queen Bee was right. Once he started he couldn't finish.

'Oi used to chase them 'prentices with an axe and nibbled theer ears if they done zummat wrong at werk.' He ground his uneven teeth together in a side-to-side motion and laughed uproariously, the race forgotten already.

Danny began to fret. The round of introductions seemed to last a lifetime; the room had begun to spin again and he felt as if he was about to pass out. He excused himself in the middle of a monologue about ferrets and stood alone outside the kitchen for five precious minutes and gulped in the frozen air. Three rabbits and a brace of pheasants were hanging upside-down on the fence, their sightless eyes stared impassively back at him in the lamplight: freeze-dried crumbs of frost and snow flecked their feathers and fur. From the direction of the garden there came the clang and gurgle of a chain-pulled toilet.

'Ah! So, *you're* Ellie's latest boyfriend,' said a bulky snow-framed silhouette. There was no escape.

He went back into the mayhem just in time to hear a voice cry out, 'Let's go to the Wonky Donkey for a game of arrows.'

'Tell those children to mind that drive. The Old Man forgot to salt it and it's iced over,' said the Queen Bee accusingly. It was said as if Dimple wasn't in the room.

The whole entourage, apart from the Queen Bee, the sleeping baby and Dimple poured into the night. The kids screamed and threw snowballs, the adults shouted at the top of their lungs.

'Mum, our Peegee put ice down my back.'

'Behave, Peegee, or I'll take you home!'

'It warn't me, it were Rufus and she knows it.'

Peegee was grabbed by the arm and shaken until his bottom lip stuck out like a shelf but a trip to the pub aged nine was not to be missed, even if it meant having to sit in the freezing porch with a flat lemonade and a packet of soggy crisps.

'Don't worry, Peegee, I'll get you some nuts,' said Danny.

'Theo always bought me pork scratchings.'

A plume of frosted breath stealthily stalked the roistering, singing, hooting, throng as they were guided to their destination down the centre of the deserted road by the iced tyre tracks of the last car to find its way home hours before.

***

Danny bought his peace offerings onto the porch of The Wonky Donkey where Peegee was sitting alone in the cold looking satisfied with his misery. He sighed heavily at times and his breath came out in short frozen huffs. The rest of the kids could be heard shouting from somewhere in the dark of the garden.

'I know I'm not as fab as your best mate, Theo, but I'll try my best. See? Scratchings instead of crisps and a pint of lemonade instead of a half. I know it's not much but it's a start.'

The boy looked at the olive branch with disdain.

'Gissa sip of your beer,' he demanded.

'No, you don't want to get started on this stuff at your age.'

'Yes I do. Go on. Just one.'

'Okay, just a small one.'

The boy took several huge gulps, grimaced and belched into Danny's face.

'Theo used to give me a sip of his Guinness. It was a lot nicer than that,' he said and handed the half-emptied glass back to its dismayed owner.

'I thought he might.'

'Got any fags?'

Danny laughed.

'What's funny?'

'You don't smoke, I hope.'

'Yeh. Alfie Stubblefield's got a paper round at Madigan's and he nicks loads of fags and swaps them for jibbers.'

He tried to grab the beer again.

Danny pulled the glass away and the boy rolled his eyes.

'People always treat me like I'm a kid.'

'That's because you are.'

'Theo always gave me more than one swig.'

'Tell me Peegee — are there any other alcoholics of your age in Sickletree or are you the only one?'

The boy just shrugged.

'Ellie told me your dad's in the air force. Do you miss him?'

'Course.'

'Where is he?'

'Germany.'

'When's he coming home?'

'How should I know? He's like everyone else in my life. They all just disappear.' He thought for a while. 'Like Theo.'

'Why do they call you, Peegee?'

''Cos they say I look like one of the monkeys off the PG Tips tea adverts.'

'No, you don't.'

'Yes I do,' and the boy pulled a chimp face with his tongue in his lower lip, scratched his armpits and beat his chest as he made grunting noises. 'They all say it.'

'Well, they say I look like one of the frogs off Pinky and Perky,' said Danny.

The boy studied him intently, head on one side.

'Yeh, you do a bit,' he said after a while.

'You're meant to say, "No, you don't".'

The boy gave another exaggerated shrug and absently opened his bag of scratchings with a trademark sigh.

'Cooee, Mr Shifter, light refreshment?' said Danny with the softest of smiles.

The boy pretended to be interested in the writing on the back of the bag of scratchings.

'Wot, no PG? Have they no taste?' retorted the boy at last and he perked up a little.

'I'm having a cup of Rosie Lee, sergeant,' said Danny.

'Can you ride tandem?' said Peegee in a fine imitation of a northern accent.

'My name is Bond, Brooke Bond,' said Danny.

'PG Tips — the tea you can really taste,' said the boy and he stuffed a handful of scratchings into his first smile of the day.

(THE BELL RINGS FOR MATINS)

Later that night Danny rose from the cushions he had pulled onto the floor from the sofa and went across the room to close the curtains. A huge full moon, held in the transcendent grip of a winter halo, lit up the surrounding woods and snowfields as if it were day. In the northern sky a spectral light shimmered in waves of purple and green. He watched transfixed as a pair of foxes danced together in the garden's drifts, raising clouds of ice crystals as they tripped the moonlight fantastic. A pair of pine trees, overgrown from distant Christmases and weighted down with snow, framed the tableau. Narnia. He went back to his improvised bed. Apart from the soft rumble of snoring, the house was silent. The fire

had died in the grate and it was bitterly cold but it was a benign, calm, cold and not the tempestuous winter storms of his past on the coast. He felt a peace he hadn't known since he was a young child. His anxiety had slowly fallen further away towards the edge of sleep when he heard soft steps.

'It's me. You okay?' she whispered.

'Yes great thanks. Haven't slept like that in years.'

'Not cold?'

'A little.'

'Sorry about the Sickletree Inquisition. I'm sure they like you but it'll take a little time for them to show it.'

'Oh, I've got time. A lifetime, hopefully.'

She quietly slipped under the blankets and gripped his arm.

'Even Wayne was calling you "Our Danny" by the end of the evening. And Peegee likes you as well, which is most unusual for him, the little monkey.'

'Only because I gave him most of my pint.'

'You did what? He's only nine you know.'

'Yeh, going on nineteen.'

'You happy?'

'Yes — very.'

'Not wishing you hadn't come up here?'

'Whatever gave you that idea?'

'Oh, nothing. It's just that you can be hard to read sometimes. You often seem on edge and I can't think why.'

'That's just me being me.'

'No need to worry with us.'

'I know. It's just the habit of a lifetime.'

She made to leave.

'Please stay,' he said.

'I can't. Dad would kill you if he found us.'

'I can't imagine Dimple killing anyone.'

'Don't be so sure. He used to chase the apprentices with —'

'— an axe. I know. He told me.'

'Well, at least you understood what he was saying.'

'Bits of it. I got the gist, anyway. Why does he limp so badly?'

'Dad was a carpenter and the work gave him arthritis. Mum says that as he created so many dodgy joints for his customers it's only fair his own joints are bad as well.'

Danny winced. 'That's a bit harsh.'

'I just came down for a quick pee and to see if you're okay — it's freezing out there.'

'I know. I've been twice already. Did it turn to ice? Mine did.'

'I'm used to it,' she said and kissed him on the cheek and slipped out from under the blankets.

'Thanks for bringing me.'

'It's my pleasure,' she said. 'The house is not up to much but we like to think *we* are.'

It occurred to him that he hadn't had anywhere to call home for a very long time.

'I can't tell if I'm in Pop Larkin's place or Cold Comfort Farm.'

'I think there's a bit of both in any home don't you? As long as we all look out for each other, then nothing else really matters, does it?'

'Well, I wouldn't know about that, would I?'

'You will.'

'It's weird. I feel as if I've been born again. Thank you.'

'You, my friend, are more than welcome.' And she was gone.

II / LAUDS

DAWN.

APPROXIMATELY 5AM

BUT VARIES

SEASONALLY.

THE ADOLESCENT

Kate's Cottage

THEY HAD BOUGHT THE cottage with an impulsive desperation. No jerry-built redbrick box on a soulless estate for them but rather good stout stone walls that had stood the test of time and mopheads of hydrangeas around the rickety garden gate. But the old world charm had come at a price. Kate's Cottage was in a poor state and decrepit to the point of being a slum. The fiscal reality of their purchase had sunk in as well and they now fully understood the implications of the £5977 they had borrowed on a ninety percent mortgage and that had only been made possible because Ellie had touched the kind heart of the mortgage assessor in her pregnant and vulnerable state. Consequently, they were tied for life. Well, twenty-five years at least and for people who up until now had always lived for the day, this was a frightening prospect. They had bought into the system and left their youth and irresponsibility behind, had become parents and it was all rather depressing and overwhelming.

There was the kitchen for example — a plank nailed to a wall as a worktop and a cracked white stone trough for a sink. No plaster on the walls, no shelves, no oven, (that was yet another thing to be bought with money they didn't have). No heating apart from a single open fire and an electric heater that was too expensive to use for longer than five minutes to take the edge off the penetrating chill. No furniture, no utensils, no bed linen, (no problem as there wasn't a bed), no car. Just plenty of nothing. If they'd actually had the metaphorical two brass farthings to rub together they would have felt better off than they actually were. In hock to the building society for a fortune, their meagre savings swallowed up by the down payment and with thousands needed spending on their home they were financially bereft with only a hollow, decomposing shell of a building with rising damp and dry rot to show for their commitment.

If he had been a pragmatist then buying the cottage would have made more sense, but he wasn't. In his life to date, he hadn't attempted even a single task that could remotely be considered practical and he had conveniently convinced himself instead that practicality was boring. He had tried reading *Zen And The Art Of Motorcycle Maintenance* which allegedly said otherwise but he had got nowhere with it; he found the Zen bits interesting but not the bikes and certainly not the engines. He was a dreamer, he knew that much and he desperately needed to snap out of his indulgent reverie and get on with his life but that required a talent and a mental strength that he didn't believe he had. And there was another problem — a massive one. His mental health had been poor for years and the added anxiety of becoming a parent, the only breadwinner of the family and the owner of an expensive slum was making it worse. He was worried sick with self-imposed pressure and the downward spiral became increasingly unbearable.

Every night, as 03:33 clicked onto the radio alarm, he woke with a start in a cold sweat and lay awake in those endless hours before dawn, obsessively checking the time, worried that unless he got a good night's rest he wouldn't be able to function properly at work during the coming day. And so, the distress took him downwards ever more rapidly as insufficient sleep fueled his anxiety. This catch-22 brought him to the end in no time and what little control he felt he had over his life disappeared completely.

The issue climaxed when he had gone into work and the panic had taken hold again, so badly this time that he almost lost control of himself. Running from the building he darted into the car park where he slumped, trembling and sweating against the wall, his heart beating itself out of his chest. He can't die — who would look after them? Certainly not his parents, they had shown no interest in them at all.

From there, his panic had taken him home and he met her at the garden gate where they had said goodbye not an hour before. She looked apprehensively at him and held the baby tightly.

'What's happened?'

'I can't do it Ellie, I feel awful.'

'Can't do what?'

'Work of course,' he said irritably. 'I keep panicking and don't know why. I feel like I'm dying.'

She looked concerned and put her hand on his arm. The baby reached out a hand and he smiled radiantly at Danny without a care in his world.

'The doctor won't give me any more tablets. He says they've got me addicted to them and that it's his job to get me off them. Bastard. He says that I'm an addict but the only drugs I've ever taken are the ones *they've* given me.'

'I know. Just do it bit by bit, hour by hour.'

'How the hell do I do that?'

'You need a project,' she said. 'It'll help you heal. We haven't the money to do the place up yet but you're a clever man and you need something to occupy your mind.'

'Where do I get the money for a hobby for Christ's sake?'

'Not all hobbies need money. We'll have a think.'

'I feel like a piece of shit.'

'You're not. You're just having a bad spell.'

'Bad spell? That's one way to describe it.'

Danny turned away from the gate and without another word got back in the car and drove away to face down his demons once more. He had discovered there was nowhere left to run and that recognition had given him the courage of desperation.

That evening after supper he wandered into the garden and the tranquility of a late summer twilight. He had hardly been in the place since they had moved in earlier that dazzling summer. In the distance, a row of hills, parched into a beige dullness and stripped of vegetation, circled the edge of town. The harvest was in early, though Danny wouldn't have known that. A solitary blackbird whistled his evening song. The open countryside started over the road which made Kate's Cottage the first and last house in that part of Sickletree, with all the beauty and peace that entailed. He looked over the stone wall to the fields beyond where he could see a fluffle of rabbits enjoying the cooling air and that reminded him of why they had fallen in love with the cottage in the first place.

He sat by the crumbling shed with his head on the cool mossy stone and looked over the garden through half-closed eyes. Against the damp wall were feathered fronds of what he took to be a decorative plant. Imagine his surprise when he saw "Asparapiss" written in a shaky hand on a ice cream stick that had been stuck into the earth next to it. Danny had never eaten asparagus but he knew it didn't look like this plant: a mystery that piqued his interest. The garden was roughly the size of an allotment — much bigger than the cottage itself but in the same poor order. The old shepherd who had owned the cottage before them had not been in good enough health to maintain it in his latter years but it retained the echoes of much love and attention in better days. A World War One tin helmet had been placed on a stick to act as a bird scarer and it rattled its rusty way to oblivion on the soft evening breeze. It articulated that through this flippant gesture the old man had symbolically cast the horrors of his former life away and begun the next one as easily as a butterfly shedding a chrysalis. Sitting there in the depths of his misery Danny found this totally inspiring.

There was the smell of nightsoil in the earth which, again, was comforting. He thought of the number of times the old man would have walked down the uneven path to dump the contents of his guzunder into the earth, then had his breakfast and got on with his daily cycle, presumably walking the fields with his dog and tending the sheep. Slowly the puzzle came together in his frazzled brain. Life was a cycle. What was it they sang at school? "After the sun the rain, after the rain the sun" or something like that. "This is the way of life 'til the work be done". Was it really that simple? He rose wearily to his feet and with a desperate religiosity prayed to a God he wasn't convinced was there. Please listen for a second, he asked. Just give me some direction and a little bit of strength.

His Nan had been a gardener; he still had a mental image of her in the extensive garden of her council house when he was a small boy. Four-foot nothing, black wellies and a Woodbine in her mouth that was staining her yellowed moustache ever darker, she was busy forking spuds from the ground. Behind her a narrow brook ran through willows and down to the sea.

"Come on Danny, these spuds won't wash themselves and they'll all be home for dinner soon". He remembered a copy of *Country Bizarre* he had treasured with its articles on folk remedies made from herbs, wild foods and the healing powers of vegetables and fruit. Practicality might not be as boring as it first seemed.

A few weighty raindrops began to fall and he squinted at the sky. It was the first time it had rained in months. He stuck out his tongue and savoured the precious drops; they tasted metallic and smelt of electricity. The rain turned into a steady downpour but he stayed in the garden and gratefully let the warm streams seep into his clothes. After the sun the rain. He laughed. 'Thanks for the message, Nan,' he shouted to the heavy grey clouds and the water running down his face blended into the tears.

In the unfurnished living room, later that evening, they unpacked a solitary tea chest of possessions from their previous life. Hidden in the bottom was a wine bottle filled with a liquid the colour of a flamingo's wing. On a torn label, stuck to the bottle with Sellotape, "My Finest Rose Petal Wine — Summer 1971" was written in an old lady's hand. They toasted Nan and shared the wine, drinking down the liquid memories from tea cups until the bottle was dry. It was as strong and sweet as a fine sherry and it tasted like nectar, falsely perhaps, but then good memories often are.

***

Their first winter at Kate's Cottage was terrible; the worst on record for years. The snows had arrived promptly in early December and lingered well into the spring with all the tenacity and insensitivity of an unwanted guest. Getting himself into work was a nightmare, emotionally as well as physically, but he managed — just.

The cottage was sparsely furnished and always freezing; the decayed windows constantly leaked the winter air and they seemed to be forever ill with bugs, chills and the snots. One particularly virulent throat lurgy laid them all up at the same time and they cuddled together in one small bed struggling to keep the shivers at bay with each other's warmth. Most worryingly, the boy seemed to be constantly ill and often struggled with his breathing. But he flourished well enough and like his mother, he was a contented soul and his smile helped them through those bleak winter months. Three times a day he sat in front of a popping log fire in his little blue dining chair, mixed his meals by hand and shovelled the mess into his fattening face with his grubby fingers and steadily grew.

And Danny had also found some strength from somewhere. His workplace was doing well and he was offered regular overtime which freed up a little cash for home improvements. Christmas was meagre that year but some cheer was brought into the home with a huge pine that Danny had chopped down and dragged from the nearby Sicklewood late on Christmas Eve. The tree was too tall for the room and Danny crudely sawed off the top to get it to fit. They stayed up to the small hours to decorate it with home-made paper chains and a silver foil star as a treetopper. In the morning the wonder on the little boy's face when he saw the tree with his meagre handful of presents underneath was heartbreaking. The little family spent the whole day sitting by the threadbare edifice, uplifted by a roaring fire and wrapped in layers of clothing while the silent snow drifted ever-deeper against the door. They lit a candle, sang carols, taught the boy nursery rhymes, read him fairy tales and got what seasonal cheer they could from the simple things in life. In later years they were to remember it as one of the best Christmases ever. In the Boxing Day sales they bought a cheap flat-pack kitchen for a few hundred pounds and Danny watched helplessly as his overconfident and waspish neighbour, Cedric, clumsily installed it on a grim day in January when a blizzard had prevented them from getting into work. Ellie took pride in choosing the cheap tiles and curtains as Danny handed Cedric the tools. It was a slow beginning but a beginning nonetheless.

***

After several false dawns the snows finally melted into the ridge and furrow meadows and spring arrived at last. In the shed, Danny found treasure — the old shepherd's worm-eaten set of garden tools — a spade, hoe, rake and fork. And so, one Saturday morning he set about turning over the fecund black soil as he removed the ranks of broad bean haulms and cabbage stems that had been left in the ground from a previous season. He built a towering bonfire and the smoke billowed away on the sharp breeze, smelling as pungent and heady as cannabis. The fragrance reclaimed memories of a lonely and ineffectual boy scout, sleeping out under lambent stars and hiking the dusty pine-needle trails of summers long past.

'You should have done that last autumn,' said a disembodied voice from the road beyond the garden wall.

'Didn't have the time, Cedric.'

'You won't get them clods ready fer planting now. You'll have to bash 'em down with yer spade. It'll take forever and a day and that's another year buggered. I did tell you to do it in the autumn, didn't I? Let the weather do the work.'

'No matter. It'll give me something to do.'

'Summat to do? Waste of time and energy,' said the old man and he sniffed. 'Quite honestly, I'm sick to death of showing people the right way to do things and then being bloody well ignored.'

'Sorry, Cedric.'

'Needed mucking as well,' he offered as a parting shot.

'Piss off, you nosy old sod,' muttered Danny to himself when he thought Cedric had gone.

'I heard that. Incidentally, I've left a bottle of Vi's parsnip wine and a sack of spuds with Ellie.'

'Thanks Cedric,' shouted Danny gratefully.

'And Harry Limerick says you can have a couple of pigeons.'

***

That spring Danny regularly took the little boy down the lane to watch the tractors working the burgeoning fields; the machines were usually followed by flocks of hysterical birds that added to the drama of the scene. The boy would stare in silent wonder at the spectacle, totally obsessed with the huge machines and even more so by the man who drove them. On these excursions he always wore his orange baby-wellies in tribute to "Fammajon" as he hero-worshipped this son of the soil in place of his useless father. This was all fine — Danny was quite happy to have the pressure taken off him by the boy being infatuated by another man. It was when his stinky wellies had to be removed at the end of the day that the real problems began.

'No, no! Fammajon weybooson.' (Farmer John has his wellie boots on).

'But Farmer John takes them off at night because he has to go to sleep.'

'No, no, no, pease! Fammajon weybooson.' He started his heartfelt sobbing and rolled around in distress.

'But Farmer John couldn't sleep wearing his wellies could he?'

'Fammajon weybooson.'

'Not all the time, little man.'

‘Yes, Fammajon weybooson.’

‘Look son, Mum’s out working and I’m in charge. It’s been a long day. These wellies are coming off.’

‘Fammajon weybooson, pease.’

‘Your feet will go manky and they’ll drop off.’

‘Fammajon weybooson.’

Later that night, before Ellie got home from work, Danny crept upstairs and carefully prized the filthy boots off the sleeping boy’s feet. He then put them outside the back door alongside the dirty nappy that he had amateurishly changed earlier that evening.

(THE BELL RINGS FOR LAUDS)

Very early, one fresh morning a little later that spring, Danny wandered into the garden just as the first light of the sun peeked into the Windrush Valley and illuminated an enormously vacant sky and the surrounding hills with a radiant glow. A huge moon counterbalanced the rising sun as it disappeared over the opposite horizon. It was then and there that he witnessed a miracle that would change his life forever. The week at work had been frantic and he’d paid no attention to the vegetable plot since the previous weekend but nature had gone about her mysterious work without him all the same. Sitting proudly in the dark soil, Danny saw to his unspeakable joy that the single neat row of broad bean seeds, donated by Cedric, that he had dropped like tiny pebbles into the cold earth in patterns of five some weeks before, had pushed their way, two leaves at a time, into existence. To Danny it was like the dawn of creation lit by the holy light of that perfect first-ever morning of the world. They were the first things he had ever grown and not one in the neat row of plants had failed. They cried out to him in unison in squeaky broad bean voices, “Oi, Danny.

It was you what did this, mate". He'd played his part in the miracle and he was welcomed, whole and happy into an embrace from Mother Nature that was to last a lifetime. Nan smiled down from above, flicked the ash off her Woodbine, signalled her appreciation with a curt nod and resumed her celestial digging.

He ran back into the cottage and without saying a word, steered Ellie up the garden path after first making her cover her eyes with her hands.

'Ta-ra!'

'There you go,' she said. 'You're not so useless after all.'

'I guess I'm not.'

'Apart from always throwing the boy's dirty nappies out the back instead of putting them in the wash.'

'They're good for deterring rodents.'

'Hmm. And those shelves you put up, fell off the wall and nearly killed him.'

'It was the rotten plaster.'

'And you did let him fall down that drain hole when you took him for that walk in the field.'

'Lucky that it was only two feet deep.'

'As I said, apart from that you're not so useless after all.'

***

Inspired by his horticultural epiphany, Danny became infatuated. Every spare moment he had he was either working overtime, watching Cedric improve the cottage or working in the garden. Before bed he read and reread the dog-eared book on vegetable gardening that the Queen Bee had bought him from a car boot sale and he kept the holy tome on his bedside table as precious as a Gideon bible. His guru was the bluff tyke, Geoffrey Smith and his no-nonsense gardening programme — a proper horny-handed man of the land who did all of his own manual work as well as dispensing pearls of vegetable wisdom in every sentence. Danny whistled the annoyingly catchy theme tune of *The Good Life* on his way to work in the garden; he saw himself as the Richard Briers character and Ellie as the lovely Felicity Kendall who had turned their back on society's fascination with materialism. It was even in front of *Fawlty Towers* on his weekly must-view list. He was always exhausted, never had a moment to spare but he had found his life's purpose in his little cottage, growing family and prolific garden. His row to redemption was planted with good intent.

***

Some years later they were sat together on a small square lawn at the top of the garden in the late autumn sunshine. Inside a cheap plastic greenhouse the last tomatoes of summer were stubbornly refusing to ripen. Danny noted that they would make some very nice chutney to add to their winter stores.

On the shelves in the kitchen were crocks of runner beans, salted and neatly laid in layers, jars of pickled cucumber, gherkins and beetroot and strings of onions hung in the French style from hooks in the ceiling. There was every variety of preserves and jams wedged into every available space throughout the cottage. In the old stone shed were hessian sacks stuffed with potatoes and stacks of huge carrots stored in cool sand in the drawers of an old sideboard. The Newton Wonder had fruited well that season with a bounty of burnished apples that would store until the following April. In the ground were leeks, turnips, parsnips, celeriac and swedes — more than enough for a hundred winter stews, soups and casseroles. The sprouts, cabbages, spinach, purple sprouting and cauliflowers would last them through the lean winter months as well. They sipped melissa tea made from lemon balm picked from Ellie's herb garden which, according to *Folk Medicine* by Dr Jarvis, would help them to live forever. A stack of freshly split wood, head high in places, was their insurance against the certainty of another hard winter to come.

The boy in a new pair of orange wellies toe-poked a ball between the runner bean canes and shouted "goal" as he fell to the ground with his arms in the air.

'*Oi!* Keep that ball off the garden please, young man.'

'And Peter Withe scores for the Villa,' shouted the boy, ignoring his father and grinning.

The toddler in the baby bouncer raised one hand in celebration and shouted "goooool" in salute to his big brother.

'I saw a house for sale in town today,' she said.

'Where?'

'In Green Lane.'

'And?'

'An old Victorian place. Three big bedrooms apparently, with a nice garden. Bit decrepit looking from the outside but loads of potential. You must know it? Old Mrs Mulgrew's place. The one that died in the spring.'

'You seem to know a lot about it.'

'I popped into the estate agent and got the details.'

'Oh, really? Where is this heading?'

'Well, you've been acting a bit bored lately and I think you need another project.'

He smiled to himself and nodded.

'How much?'

'More than we can afford but that didn't stop us before.'

'Is there a vegetable garden?'

'There's more important things than your spuds to worry about. School, shops, doctors, buses, there's all those things to consider as well as the house itself. We can't stay stuck out here on the edge of town now the boys are bigger.'

'Is there a vegetable garden?' repeated Danny with a smile.

'There's a Co-op five minutes away with some lovely sprouts.'

'Is there a vegetable garden?'

'No, but there's the God's Acre allotments just down the lane. I went to the council offices and put your name down for a plot. So, you get two projects for the price of one. Lucky you, eh?'

'Really?'

'I thought that I'd better get a move on as there's a very long waiting list.'

'You're serious aren't you.'

'Yes. What do you think?'

Danny sat and pondered. He'd miss his garden for sure but not that damp, cold cottage. The garden had done its job and had been there when it was needed, like an old friend who picks you up when you're hitching alone on the road. Maybe it *was* time to move on.

'I am thinking, can we rise to the occasion again?'

'Well, we do have a good track record of meeting a challenge, so it's pretty much a sure-fire cert we can do it again.'

'You don't hang about do you.'

'Someone else is probably looking at it at this very moment.'

Danny looked down the garden. After the sun the rain, after the rain the sun. He made a mental note to leave the tin helmet for the next owner. He was sure the old shepherd would have wanted it that way.

III / PRIME

EARLY MORNING.

THE FIRST HOUR

OF DAYLIGHT.

APPROXIMATELY 6AM.

THE YOUNG MAN

The Prophet of the Sicklewood

HE PICKED UP HIS fishing tackle and angrily slammed the front door of the cottage despite the fact that the sun had barely risen and the world was still sleeping. The noise echoed off down the street but, selfishly, he didn't care one bit. Things had been tough at home recently and he was on the edge — there was a fire in his head and he needed some space and the right place to think to try to make sense of what was going on. He strode the narrow dirt track which ran parallel to the Roman Road and along the complete length of the Happy Valley. Tumuli, tree circles and sheep, were scattered on the pristine hills like abandoned stones, their transient shadows stretched by the early morning sun. The wind stirred rippling green oceans of grass and a squall of thistledown crossed his path but he paid none of this solitary beauty any mind. He missed several more irreplaceable moments of serendipity as the raging conversation in his head became ever more hysterical with every step he took.

With his focus elsewhere it seemed no time at all before he was standing on the edge of a primordial woodland. Here he stopped to reconnect with nature, placed his fishing rod over his shoulder and let the trees enfold him within their healing embrace.

Beneath the canopy the world was in a half-light, so dark that Danny had to grip a handrail of twisted branches until he became accustomed to the gloom. For some time he followed an indistinct, twisting pathway that led to a curving stairway of broken stone steps which had been awkwardly set into the earth like a jaw filled with mossy, worn teeth. This slippery ladder led up to a giant's maze of tumbled boulders through which he carefully threaded his way, cursing himself for not leaving a trail on his last visit months before. The Sicklewood didn't give up its secrets willingly. Tangled roots like gnarled witchfingers grasped at his unsuspecting feet and ankles and slimy logs, intended to serve as stepping stones across muddy pools and brooks, only added to the wood's malicious treachery. Just the young and nimble had best stray this way.

If Danny had been a newcomer to the Sicklewood it would have been easy to become lost in the intricate maze of paths that criss-crossed each other as the wood pulled the wanderer ever closer to its sacred heart. Trees mockingly pointed in a thousand different directions, deceitful rabbits led travellers up the garden path to who knows where and even a gentle deer could sometimes appear threatening. But he knew where he was and how to get where he wanted to be and he followed nature's signposts with care in the knowledge that if he missed one and took a wrong turn it would take an age to find his way back to his starting point. The only other living things in here apart from himself — the trees, small animals, birds and insect life — were not about to help him in one of the few domains where they still reigned supreme. He followed the directions of the sycamore with a dead branch, twigged at the end like a pointing hand and stepped carefully over an infirm bridge that traversed a dank gorge and its sluggish runnel.

There was only the fitful rattle of a woodpecker to be heard as he arrived in a clearing, no more than thirty yards across, where the trees had been cleared for no apparent purpose many years before; their petrified stumps circled the arena like a ring of prehistoric stones. An owl on his late way home from a night's hunting floated silently across the glade — from darkness into light and back into darkness — a lifetime in a moment. It was in this hallowed space, where the misted and enchanted Windrush cut a platinum ribbon through the Sicklewood, that he sat amongst the rainbow of fungi that was devouring a fallen giant and unpacked his fishing gear. As he worked, a viper in its enamelled skin watched him attentively from her bed of leaf, bone and scale, before uncurling and going about her day.

(THE BELL RINGS FOR PRIME)

Danny pushed through a stand of teasels at the water's edge and cast his line into the swirling water. He then sat back on his haunches into a bank of ramblers, oxlips, wild thyme and sweet-smelling honeysuckle and stared abstractedly at the end of his line. Why was she being so difficult? He was doing his best but that never appeared to be good enough. She seemed angry and critical of him and that was so unlike her. Okay, he knew that one of his many faults was that he took things too personally but she was his wife, so how was he meant to take it? Brush off the criticism? He'd never been able to do that. So, instead of tackling the problem head on and talking it through, he had decided to sulk and take off at every opportunity and that was what he was doing today. If she didn't want him around then he'd gladly oblige.

Starting from his painful reverie as the float bobbed twice, he leapt to his feet and slowly reeled in his line. The end of the rod bent alarmingly as he fought to land the fish until finally they lay gasping together on the bank, the age-old drama complete.

Danny was struggling with the fire — all smoke and no flame. It was quiet apart from the music of the Windrush, a solitary cuckoo and Danny's muted swearing which had become ever more inventive as the fire refused to take hold. He was fully occupied by his task, which was all well and good as he was not looking forward to despoiling the beautiful rainbow trout that stared at him reproachfully from glazed eyes.

It was above this green noise that Danny heard the crack of a twig and his heart leapt into his chest. At the opposite end of the clearing, almost completely camouflaged by trees and looking as wild as an Old Testament prophet, stood a hooded man. They studied each other for some time before the older man moved towards the fire. He wore a battered army tunic the colour of dead moss, a heavy piece of cloth wrapped around his head for a hood and what looked like a pair of tartan bedroom slippers coated in mud. His filthy feet were sockless. Wild hair and a grey beard, which covered half of his face, accentuated a pair of mesmerising green eyes. When he spoke it was apparent that he had lost most of his teeth as he whistled his esses.

'You're doing that fire all wrong, son. I can fix it — that is if you don't mind of course.'

'Yes, sure. Please do.'

'I'm Jack Green. I lives in the Sicklewood.'

'I'm Danny Hucklesby. I live in Sickletree.'

They shook hands. The old man's handshake was as light and feeble as a small bundle of twigs; his fingers rustled like dry leaves as Danny firmly squeezed his hand but there was a light in his eyes above his bristle-brush beard that belied his apparent age. He smelt of damp earth, woodsmoke and bark, that is, of the Sicklewood.

Green pulled what looked like a ball of cotton wool from deep within his shabby clothing, lit the ball with embers from Danny's fire and blew on it until it was smoking heavily. He then bent down and put the ball into the heart of the dying fire and in no time the smoke had been replaced by a blaze.

'Plenty o' practice,' he said. 'Now then. What about that little silver darling — may I?'

He gutted the fish with a small knife he had produced from his army belt and placed it over the fire on a sharpened stick where it began hissing and spitting in no time. The entrails were dropped back into the river where he washed his hands.

'Send its heart back to the Windrush where it belongs,' he said and he made the sign of the cross. 'Every crittur has a purpose and a soul.'

He was soon on to more secular matters.

'Got to cook 'em slowly, they tastes better when some of the fat comes out. And not too close or else they burns on the outside and stays raw on the inside. Fuckin' 'orrid then they are.'

'Okay, cheers,' said Danny. He thought for a moment about offering his guest a drink from his flask but decided against it.

'Oh, wait a minute,' said Green and he pulled a large handful of live crayfish with their claws bound by rubber bands from a pocket of his miraculously productive battledress.

He made the sign of the cross once more and threw them into the fire.

'Most boils them in salt water but I likes them best like this.' The crayfish hissed their disapproval.

'It's great in here isn't it? What a wonderful place to think.'

Green put an unsanitary finger to his lips to indicate to Danny to shush. 'Yeh, don't keep on,' he said impatiently to nobody in particular. The poor old sod's hearing voices thought Danny.

'I talks to the critturs and trees. After all this time in here I sort of gets what their gabbling on about. It's just gossip mainly. Or the weather. They're asking who you are.'

'Oh, really?' said Danny, feeling strangely honoured.

'I lives with the badgers and elves. Oh, don't laugh. They're in here alright if you knows where to look. The badgers I means, the elves were a joke — though sometimes I wonders.' His voice tailed off and he paused before shaking his head.

Danny turned the sizzling fish and let him continue.

'Did you know the Romans were in here? They loved the place. Their mine shafts are everywhere. It's them that caused that maze of boulders you came through. Oh, yes, I was watching you all the way in. See that earth bank over there by those hazels? That's a Roman fort. When the legions camped for the night they would clear a square in the trees and throw up an earth palisade with the sharpened stakes on top. Imagine doing that in a different place every night? At least *our* trenches stayed put — they never moved an inch in years. They say there are still trees alive in here that witnessed druid sacrifices. Course, I don't know if that's true — you'll have to ask *him*.' He indicated a gnarled oak whose roots poked from the earth like an arthritic hand reaching for the light.

'You said you live in here. Do you mind me asking why?'

'Come in here during the Second War to avoid conscription. I was that unfortunate age you see. Born at the end of the last century, so I was unlucky enough to serve in the First and still young enough to serve in the Second. So, I wasn't going to wait around to see if I'd be invited to join in their second shitshow. Course, back then the Sicklewood was bigger — it was the size of half of the county. It's much smaller now but people still keeps out of here because of its reputation.'

His voice became hoarse and he began to cough.

'I was never right after Passchendaele — gas and shell shock it was. Cowardice they called it and they had me arrested. Called me a fucking malingerer and gave me a fine kicking, but they had shot so many of us by then that they'd made their point and they didn't press charges. Even those butchers in the red caps were sick of the carnage.' He laughed sardonically. 'But I warn't doing it again. No way. I says me goodbyes to Jess and the Little'un and legged it in here in double-quick time. For forever as it turned out.'

Danny took the fish off the fire and poked it with his finger.

'Needs a little bit more time, me boy.'

'How are your family now?'

'Wouldn't know. I keeps away from the world. Been in the Sicklewood since thirty-nine. What year is it now?'

'It's 1976.'

'Really? Well, then I haven't seen them for thirty-seven years.'

'But, they're most probably both still alive.'

Green had shown no emotion when he spoke of his family. If he had any affection left for them he either covered it well or, more likely, those feelings had long since died. Perhaps his wartime experiences had meant that there had never been any true bond in the first place; how else to explain he had stayed that close geographically but had never gone back, if what he said was true.

'I don't think they'd want to see me anyways. Don't forget that I abandoned them. I left them alone in wartime to fend for themselves. I'm pretty sure they wouldn't want to see me,' he repeated flatly. He shrugged his shoulders and turned the fish over. 'Best not to pick at old wounds, eh? You'll find that in this life doing that will get you sweet Fanny Adams. Besides, someone had to protect the trees. Those greedy bastard developers moved in, so I'd sabotage their machines when they came a-cuttin' them beauties down to find the space to build their roads and box-houses. As I said, you can't imagine how huge this place was back then. My army training helped me to stay out of sight and put some spanners in their works. I think they thought it was just kids draining their tanks and flattening their tyres. But they kept a-coming. Nothing could stop their greed.'

'Didn't they come looking for you?'

'I heard some voices shouting my name after the war ended. But it was easy to avoid them. They made a lot of noise tramping through the place.'

'How do you get by without any company?'

'You sees all sorts in here. Lovers, ramblers, scientists — even suicides. I keeps away from them all, especially those who wants to finish it. I seen enough save Jerry a bullet in all sorts of ways in the war for it to worry me. My way of looking at it is, if someone *does* want to finish it, that's their business. Been to that door many times myself, but never had the guts to flip the latch.'

'Don't you ever wish you could go back?'

'I likes it in here. Besides, where's the magic in *your* world?'

'Magic?'

'Yeh, magic. England was Arcadia when I was a young man. It was *full* of magic. Now the money and machines have destroyed it and it's all about noise, greed and tearing things up. People have stopped looking for the magic.'

'Arcadia? I don't know what you mean.'

'You can't really describe what it means but I'll try. It's when you walks across a summer field at dusk and you hear the call of a barn owl. He's talking to you — did you know that? Or when the first flake from a steel sky settles onto the branches of a winter elm.

Or when you sees a March hare shadow-boxing in a spring meadow. Or a starry autumn night when a low crescent moon is over the Windrush and the trout takes a fly. Ah, you can't really describe it to someone who's never known it. But I knows, mate, I knows! Have you ever read *The Wind in the Willows*?'

'Several times.'

'Well, you should know what I means then. It's all in there. It's in the small moments of life. There's still a little of Arcadia left in the Sicklewood but it's shrinking by the day. And when it's gone it'll be for ever. The magic'll never return once it's lost.'

'Okay then. If, as you say, the magic has gone why not go home? It might be there with your family.'

'But that's just the point. There is still some of that magic left in here. That's what I said, didn't I? The Sicklewood's a magical place and so peaceful. I sleep the sleep of ages every night and there's plenty of free food to be had. I nicks a few eggs from the farms and catches a few critturs in me traps. Squirrel stew with wild garlic is me favourite. And grilled trout.' He looked hungrily at the sizzling fish and gave out a throaty woodsmoke chuckle.

'Do you want it?'

'You sure?'

'Absolutely. It wouldn't be cooked if you hadn't helped me.'

Green pulled a small bag of wild herbs from his chest pocket and sprinkled them over the fish. He demolished the trout down to the bones in no time before savouring the fatty skin which he took an age to chew before swallowing. The crayfish he lifted from the fire with the stick and cracked the claws open on a stone. His lips smacked as he worked a solitary tooth away at the pink and white flesh. After he was done and had wiped his greasy hands on his trousers, Danny found a packet of sweets in his bag. He offered them to Green who regarded them as if they were made of gold.

'You sure?' he asked again. His eyes watered up.

'Very sure,' said Danny.

'I haven't had a sweet in years. I remembers having one that someone dropped in the mud once. It was lovely.'

'Well, I can fetch you anything that you want from the town. Anything. Any time. Just name it.'

'No, it's okay, thanks,' said the old man as he painfully rose to his feet. 'Best be on me way.'

'Don't be daft. A few treats never hurt. If you don't want to meet up I'll leave them by that dead log over there.'

'I said no, didn't I?'

'Fair enough, Mr Green,' said Danny to himself as he watched the old man melt back into the Sicklewood.

***

'Where youse bin, Dad?' said the toddler as he wrapped his arms around Danny's leg. 'I missed you.'

Danny ruffled his thick mop of blond hair.

'Cup of tea, love?' said Ellie from the sink.

'Yes, please.'

'Are you okay?'

'Yes thanks. Sorry I went off like that but I needed some space.'

'I know, but please don't go off without telling me where you're going in future. I've been worried sick.'

'I won't.'

'The boy missed you badly. He was frightened you weren't coming home.'

She put her hands on his shoulders, kissed him on the cheek and stood back and studied his face. An unconditional forgiveness was one of her many qualities.

‘I was just about to send out a search party.’

‘Well, there’s a coincidence. Talking of search parties, I met an old fella in the woods who was on the run from the authorities, or so he believed. Jack Green.’

‘It couldn’t have been him.’

‘It was definitely him, he told me his whole story about the war, all about his family and how he’d become some sort of ecological warrior in his later years, fighting against The Man and his destructive works.’

‘It couldn’t have been him because they found him hanging in the woods years ago. It was in all the papers when I was a kid.’

Danny was shocked into a long silence.

‘Well, maybe the bloke they found wasn’t him.’

‘He was identified by his daughter, Emily. His wife had died.’

‘Well, now I know you *are* wrong because Jack Green told me he left his family when Emily was just a baby. How would she know what he looked like? I know for a fact he would have changed from any old photos she would have seen of him. You ought to see the state he’s in now.’

‘He had some personal items on him that identified him: a family photo and a ration book. And a pipe and a ring, if I remember rightly. It was definitely him, Danny. Somebody has been playing you along.’

‘Unless he planted his personal effects on somebody else. Funny, he said to me that the Sicklewood was a place for suicides and that he understood their reasons for wanting to end it all. Maybe it was just his way of finally being left alone.’

‘Well, if it wasn’t him, how come the dead person wasn’t registered as missing and identified by *his* family.’

‘I definitely saw him and spoke to him. He was even still wearing his old uniform.’

'Surely somebody else would have seen him after all these years? I bet some other old tramp who knew Jack's story was pulling your plonker.'

'My what? Not in front of the boy please.'

'Was he pulling your plongerer?' asked the boy.

They both laughed.

'I can't follow this any more,' said Danny. 'The plot's harder to decipher than *The Wednesday Play*.'

'Well, Kojak, it's a mystery that'll probably never be solved. Do you want some brown sauce with your cheese on toast?'

'No thanks,' said Danny. 'Actually, I'm not that hungry. I had trout and crayfish for lunch.'

***

Danny walked into the Sicklewood as he did at the first hour of daylight on the same day every year. He looked for the parcel that he had left by the decaying log on his previous visit but there was nothing to be found apart from a few sweet wrappers, the damp embers of a fire and a scattering of crayfish shells which patterned the carpet of moss with pink shards of reflected sunlight. As he searched the glade the Windrush whispered its endless story to the accompaniment of rustling leaves and birdsong as if it was urgently trying to tell the young man an important secret. But he either hadn't listened carefully enough or understood its message because he turned his back to the river instead and walked away from his secluded sanctuary to live another year

IV / TERCE

MID-MORNING

PRAYER.

THIRD HOUR.

APPROXIMATELY 9AM.

THE ADULT

A Wellie Full of Water

TRAPPED BETWEEN THE SCOUT hut car park and the mill race and no more than a rotten spud's throw away from the nettle and comfrey carpeted bank of a tranquil stretch of the sleepy Windrush, two men were working in the last green space of any note left in the centre of town. In truth calling it work would be stretching it somewhat and calling it a green space would be stretching it even further as, within these tight borders a plastic, glass and wooden shanty town of sheds, polytunnels, greenhouses, raised beds and bizarre Heath Robinson constructions of every kind had sprung from the rich and mainly well-tended soil, like so many weeds. Quite how this refugee camp for the bored, harassed and dispossessed had been allowed to grow to such proportions was difficult to ascertain unless one knew that, in their elevated wisdom, the only constraints laid down by the Sickletree Town Council on construction matters in their allotment holder's agreement could be considered scanty to say the least.

Item 1: No shed is to be bigger than eight feet by six.
Item 2: No paint other than brown or green aloud (sic).
Item 3: No hazardous chemicals or materials to be used.

And even these insufficient instructions had been ignored of course, that is, if one assumed they had ever been known. Country folk were country folk and "okkord" down to the last woman and man. Consequently, ramshackle buildings of every imaginable design and hue (purples, blues, greys and even subtle shades of pink were now fashionable) had been allowed to proliferate on the site and the stockpiling of any convenient construction material, whether scrounged, stolen or bought on the cheap, was rife. Decomposed asbestos sheeting, illegally retrieved from local building sites, was a particular favourite for roofing sheds and this deadly bounty had been stacked in lethal piles around the site for potential future use. Cocktails of toxic chemicals bubbled sinisterly in large plastic containers, their exact contents and purpose either long forgotten or unknown; jagged booby traps of broken glass lurked behind sheds and planks of rotten wood, with their porcupine quills of splinters and rusted nails and screws, littered the site. Accordingly, the homespun development had grown untended like a scattering of seeds — a few of which had blossomed into beautiful flowers but the majority revealed themselves to be about as desirable and useful as squitch on a cabbage patch. No wonder that the site had recently become known as "Chernobyl" as on a grey day in winter it closely resembled the aftermath of a nuclear disaster.

The Town Council preferred to rule by proclamation and decree rather than consultation and the powers-that-be would only reluctantly venture from their cosy offices to take advantage of a rare PR opportunity or to settle one of the frequent internecine disputes between plot holders who always seemed to be spoiling for a fight. So, if you ignored the abundance of notices, badly laid out in pompous and archaic tones (*Sickletree Town Council does hereby decree etc.*) that smothered the wooden five-bar gate at the entrance, then you were not to know what the Council was dictating and proclaiming and could legitimately (or illegitimately, depending on which side of the fence you sat) plead ignorance of their regulations and directives. Other than that it seemed that anything went and the allotmenteers were pretty much left to do things their own way and in their own good time. If the God's Acre allotments in Sickletree were a child whose parents were the Council then the organisation would be held criminally responsible for abandoning and neglecting its charge.

(THE BELL RINGS FOR TERCE)

'Here, come and look at this,' said Raspberry from behind his rickety shed.

'At what?' said his co-worker.

'Two snails are having it away on this cabbage.'

'Do I have to?'

'Yes, Danny, sorry but you do. You may even learn something.'

'I'm not sure if I've ever told you this before, Raspberry, but I've never been into gastropod porn.'

'God, he's breathing heavy.'

'So would you. As he's a snail it'll probably take him all summer to reach a conclusion.'

'Judging by the look of him he won't get that far.'

'No premature ejaculation concerns for Sid the Snail then?'

'Doesn't look like it. Go on my son.'

'How do you know which one is "him"?'

'He's the one smiling and he's left his socks on.'

It was one of those gleaming autumnal days that are perfect for working on the land: warm enough for the bitter winds of winter not to ache the bones and cool enough not to sweat the brow. The season was at its most fruitful point and the glut of produce had encouraged the sin of wastefulness. Runner beans had been allowed to go to seed and unwanted courgettes had grown as fat as marrows and were regularly being fed to delighted chickens. Tomatoes had been left to rot on the vine and squashes of every size, shape and colour were being deliberately ignored. There was just too much of it all and the overloaded compost heaps had resumed their eternal journey from flourishing plant to decay and then a return to the earth in readiness for the cycle to begin all over again.

The workers stopped their efforts and sat down on makeshift chairs on the roughly-slabbed patio outside the shed. Raspberry commandeered the slightly more comfortable upturned pot and Danny was left to relax as best he could on the edge of a coldframe. The place was a hidden haven that acted as a suntrap and they needed their baseball caps to deflect the punishing glare. Behind them the mill race of the Windrush provided a burbling soundtrack to their discussion and flickering white butterflies went about their mysterious work as determined and focused as any businessman on the road to success. From here the river disappeared under the medieval stone bridge that carried the road eastward out of Sickletree and off to far bigger and more interesting places.

'What time is it going to arrive?' asked Danny.

'About lunchtime, but he's a bit unpredictable.'

'And who've you asked to help?'

'We have the Gaffer of course and I also asked Little Hands the Tomato Thief.'

'Is that it? They're both ancient. They won't last five minutes.'

'I put a note about it on the gate as well.'

'Nobody reads those notices and your writing's indecipherable anyway so I wouldn't count on that drawing any attention.'

'It's only a trailer load — it's not much and won't take long to barrow to our plots. We'll be fighting each other over the leftovers come teatime.'

'Did you leave any cones to stop the cars blocking off the gate.'

'I forgot, but it'll be fine. Stop mithering. It's only a pile of crap. Stop worrying about nothing.'

'It's only a *big* pile of crap.'

'There's a hell of a bonfire going up on the Gaffer's plot. He keeps saying he's not well so they could be cremating him,' said Raspberry, slyly getting off the subject of the delivery of manure.

'Quiet, here he comes.'

They both looked up the path to where an elderly man with a military bearing was effortlessly striding towards them carrying a large and obviously heavy bucket of potatoes.

'I wish you hadn't asked him,' muttered Danny.

'Why not? He's stronger than you and me put together.'

'Raspberry, he's nearly ninety and he always says he's ill. He might actually be right this time. What if he decides to kark it halfway through the job, what'll we do then?'

'Chuck him on his bonfire?'

'This could end up as the Great Shit Shifting Disaster of the God's Acre Allotments. Don't say anything about the manure — he'll be about as much use to us as a chocolate kettle.'

'We won't have any trouble finding somewhere to bury him — just dig a trench on your potato patch and stick him in head first.'

'He was telling me yesterday that he doesn't have long left.'

'Nonsense. He'll outlive us all. What's wrong with the world's oldest hypochondriac now?'

'He thinks he might have fowl pest.'

'Humans can't catch fowl pest.'

'He can. The Gaffer can catch anything he wants. He thinks the Sickletree area is historically prone to infection. What did he call them? Miasmas or something. He says the illnesses are carried on the breeze and that anyone can catch them at any time. Apparently, the clue can be found in the name — *Sick*-letree.'

'He's losing his marbles.'

The Gaffer strode briskly around the shed and Raspberry greeted him with a song.

'At a quarter to two, I'll know where you'll be,
Shovelling shit on the Isle of Capri.'

'At a quarter to *six*, I'll know where he'll be. *Still* shovelling shit in Sickletree,' corrected Danny.

'I saw Roland yesterday. Over by that celeriac,' said the Gaffer, ignoring Raspberry's musical introduction and pitching straight in with a new theme of conversation.

'I thought you said you'd killed him,' said Danny.

'Yep, I jumped on him and squished him last week,' said the old man with macabre relish.

'So, it was most probably a relative of his?'

'Could be.'

'They come up from the river and nick stuff, the little bastards. I had one drop on me head when I was a kid. I can still feel its little claws scratching me neck. Still have dreams about it.'

'I'm a killer,' said the Gaffer. He ignored Raspberry's anecdote and started counting a litany of death and destruction on his fingers. 'I've killed partridges, pheasants, pigeons, woodcocks, chickens, deer, badgers —'

'Yeh, thanks for the casualty list, John Wayne,' said Danny.

'— rabbits, worms —'

'Worms? They don't count, surely.'

'Yeh, worms, toads, frogs, foxes, so a little rat is no problem for a killer like me,' said the Gaffer with the pride in his work of a professional assassin.

'He's the Worminator,' said Raspberry.

'Well, it was either a resurrected Roland or one of his relatives, just so's you know. Wouldn't want him to scare you and you have to run off behind your polytunnel again, screaming like a little girl,' said the Gaffer to Danny.

'Don't worry about me,' said Danny. 'A little bird tells me that you plan to help shifting the muck.'

'That's right. And who else is coming down to help?'

'At the moment it is just us three with Little Hands the Tomato Thief to make up our merry band,' said Raspberry.

'Not that idle, thieving little bugger. I'll swear it was him that had those carrots off my plot. He'll be worse than useless anyway. He's too old.'

'He's younger than *you*,' said Danny.

'Everyone's younger than *him*,' said Raspberry.

'Only just. And I've kept meself in much better shape than he has,' said the Gaffer. 'He lives on beer and chips and I live on green tea and pheasant stew.'

'Every lifetime has a cycle. Animals, plants *and* humans. Yours is definitely at the gone-to-seed-before-being-put-on-the-compost-heap stage,' said Raspberry.

'You should *never* compost weeds,' said Gaffer. 'Never, *ever*!'

'I know. You've probably told me that fifty times before and I still do it just for a laugh and to wind you up.' Raspberry winked at Danny.

'Oh, I nearly forgot. Booty Brocklebank said he might come down for a couple of barrowloads as well. So that's another helper,' said Raspberry.

'How's that gonna work then? Last time I heard, his broken leg was still in plaster,' said Danny.

'To be fair, I told him we'd barrow it for him.'

'We? So, no other help at all then. Why even mention it? Why's he even coming down? Why doesn't he just sit at home and let us do it all for him?'

'Actually, to be honest, that is what's happening. He *is* staying at home but I'll still be able to make a tenner off him. He's desperate for some muck for his rhubarb and he'll pay anything within reason.'

'You think a fiver a barrowload is reasonable?'

'It's the law of supply and demand,' said Raspberry.

'Why don't people bloody listen? I've not got long left so you'd better take note. After me, nobody'll have The Knowledge,' said the Gaffer, interrupting the flow of conversation once more.

'Knowledge of what?' asked Danny

'Of how to do things effing properly of course. I hate seeing things done wrong. These wimmin that come down here. They've watched one episode of Alan effing Titchmarsh and think they knows the lot. I seen him on TV the other day pull a whole parsnip straight out of a bed of compost with a stupid smirk on his face. Pull it out by hand, mind. No scratches on the parsnip, not a speck of dirt on the bugger, just a complete effing parsnip looking like it's just been picked off the shelf of a supermarket, which it probably had by some dozy twat in a film crew. It's a joke and these stupid bints swallow it whole and think it's that easy. Chuck an effing seed in the ground and pull the bastard out with one hand a few months later. The reality is you've got to go halfway down to effing

Australia to get the bugger out of a trough of mud and water and then the end of the bastard thing still snaps off. It's an effing joke. No wonder they give up after a year. Too much like bloody hard work. And thanks to bloody Alan Squitchfarce they keep turning up in their droves every season like a squad of clueless Land Girls.'

'You finished?' said Danny.

'Yes.' The old man looked spent by his outburst.

'Good. Well, as a counter to that finely argued thesis I'd say Bargearse does all right — after a fashion. She's a woman — I think — almost as old as your good self and she still manages to get some good produce off her plot.'

'The bollocks she does! She never digs it! Just turns the top over with one of them bloody corkscrew things that they sell for five bob down at Gooley's and then whacks the seeds into rough ground. That's not bloody gardening is it? No wonder all her plants are in miniature. Bonzai sprouts for pity's sake. What's that all about?'

'You just didn't like it when you poked your nose in and she told you to piss off and mind your own. She used to be a university lecturer and is a well-known feminist, so she'll be much brighter than all of us put together,' said Danny.

'Not difficult,' said Raspberry. 'That just means she's got more than three brain cells.'

'Cleverer than me? She knows nothing at all about allotments. They shouldn't allow wimmin down here at all,' said the Gaffer. 'It's unlucky.'

There was a brief moment of reflection as all three considered the matter and then came to the conclusion that the discussion wasn't worth pursuing.

'Changing the subject quickly, does anyone know the weather forecast?' said Raspberry.

'Rain,' said the Gaffer. 'And heavy as well. There's a big storm coming through. I saw it on —'

'When?' interrupted Danny.

'I saw it on the morning news.'

'No. When's the *rain* due?' said an exasperated Danny.

'About now,' said the Gaffer casting a weather-beaten glance at a rapidly clouding sky.

***

'How much is here?'

'Oh,' said the farmer and he pulled a quizzical expression and scratched his stubbled chin. 'Five tons? Maybe more.'

'What we gonna do with all this, Raspberry?' asked Danny.

'I dunno mate. Stick it on yer allotment?'

'I warned you several times, that a trailer load would be far too much. It'll take us forever to shift.'

'You ordered a trailer load and that's what you got,' interrupted the farmer. 'That'll be fifty-quid towards me weekend beer money.' He held out a huge red hand, palm upwards. Raspberry obsessively counted out ten crinkled five-pound notes and handed them over with the reluctance of a seasoned miser. To the terminally mean allotmenteer it looked a huge wedge of cash and it obviously pained him to part with it.

The farmer stuffed the money into the back pocket of his filthy trousers and clambered hurriedly and awkwardly back on to his tractor. He took a last look at the huge pile of manure, shook his head and laughed out loud.

'See you next year boys,' he shouted out of the window and waved a hand as he drove away. 'You might've finished by then.'

They studied the manure. It was piled chest high, fifteen-feet across and totally blocked the entrance to the allotments in huge straw-bound clumps. The smell could peel paint. Massive flies had already begun to gather in their thousands — gigantic, ferocious blue monsters that seemed agitated rather than pleased with their windfall but who guarded it aggressively nonetheless. Danny and Raspberry then ran the rule over their ragged band of helpers whose combined ages exceeded a double century. The motley assembly of poor physical specimens leant on their shovels and stared back at them with a variety of accusatory looks and couldn't have looked less motivated by their huge mental and physical challenge if they had tried. Despondence as well as manure was in the air.

'Please, gentlemen. Wouldn't it have been much better to have dropped it inside the gate, isn't it?' observed the fifth member of the team.

'Well, if you had been here on time Ishaan, you would have known that it *had* to be dumped *outside* because some twat has left his brand new Audi right in the way and we couldn't back the trailer in.'

'But, please. Have you considered that this may be a problem, isn't it?' said Ishaan and he pointed behind the group to where six cars had been trapped in their parking spaces by the errant Audi and the heap of manure.

'Bloody hell, Raspberry — why did you let him dump it here? If any of those cars need to get out in an emergency then we're in the shit.'

'Literally in the shit, isn't it?' said Ishaan.

'I only need two barrowloads said the Gaffer. 'And I've got to get them all the way up the other end.'

'That's no excuse you old skiver,' said Raspberry. 'You'll shift your share.'

'How old are *you*?' said the Gaffer pointing a bent forefinger at Danny.

'Forty-four.'

'And *you*?' he demanded of Raspberry.

'Forty-two, next week, I think.'

'Well, that makes me more than both your ages put together. I'm eighty-eight, you know.' He said this angrily as if his advanced age was the younger men's responsibility. 'How about showing me some effing respect for once?'

'I know how old you are,' said Danny. 'It's etched into my brain for eternity. This year you must have told us both a hundred times how old you are. It's not our fault and there's bugger all we can do about it even if we wanted to.'

'I'll tell you what, Gaffer, you miserable old sod, you can have your two barrowloads but they'll still cost you a fiver each. If you remember, we agreed to split the cost equally, five-ways between us. I'm not paying for more muck than I need just because you're too old and knackered to cart any more than two barrowloads to your plot,' said Raspberry.

'No — effing — way. Fifty-pee for my little bit, or nothing. And that's being generous — that's ten bob in proper money.'

'Me too. I shan't need much either,' said Little Hands the Tomato Thief. 'And I'm eighty-six by the way. I've got to get the Missus's fish and chips home by two so we'd better stop bickering and get a move on.'

'Oh, that's effing marvellous and not what we agreed to at all. Danny and I get a huge pile of shite we don't need and have to pay through the nose for it into the bargain. Thanks very much for nothing. I organise this delivery in all good faith and get left holding the baby by two lazy old gits who are both sitting on fat pensions but who are too tight to pay what they owe.'

'Tough life innit, Razzer?' said the Gaffer abruptly. 'But you'll get over it. It'll take time but one day in the distant future you'll come to terms with it and thank us for our support.'

'We'd better get a move on,' said Little Hands the Tomato Thief. 'Look at that sky.' The first of the rain began falling in threatening drops.

'And please gentlemen. Keep off Bargearse's plot for crying out loud. I'll never hear the end of it if we run a barrow over her poxy spinach,' said Danny.

'Is there anything you don't worry about?' said Raspberry.

'Not where you're concerned, mate,' said Danny.

'Come on you wimps,' shouted Raspberry to his ragged band. 'This shit ain't gonna shift itself.'

And with that he snatched up his spade and charged single-handedly at the manure pile with all the desperate courage of a VC winner. He beat at the cloud of angry flies with the tool whilst shouting: 'Piss *off* you filthy, dirty, little *bastards*,' at the top of his voice. This seemed to do the trick and the cloud dispersed into thin air in an instant. It appeared that even flies knew a committed and dangerous foe when they encountered one and they cut their losses and flew. If you were unlucky enough to get stuck in the trenches when the bullets were flying and all seemed lost, then this tough little man, whose *modus operandi* was to face any situation as it arose with courage, good humour, calmness, fortitude and a manic determination, was exactly the type of person you'd want by your side. In no time at all his barrow was full to the brim with twice the weight that any of the others could have managed and he was blazing a speedy trail into the distance.

'Come on ladies, keep up with Raspberry,' he hollered.

***

Over five hours later Danny and Raspberry wheeled their last barrowloads on to their plots in the howling gale. Rain continued to bucket down in sheets as it had since their project had begun. The manure was plastered everywhere across the site and two brown trails blighted the grass paths to signpost where they'd trundled countless sodden loads to their destinations. A sickly smell of muck mixed with damp bonfire hung in the air. Luckily, not a single owner of a trapped car had braved the weather and therefore there had been no confrontations with irate motorists. This was most probably just as well because the patience of the labourers had been worn to breaking point and the outcome of any argument would probably only have been resolved by violence. 'Fuck 'em,' Raspberry had said. 'If anyone turns up they'll just have to wait.'

They sat exhausted by the swollen river, shielded from the worst of the rain by a row of overgrown willows and sharing the comradeship and elation that only a difficult task that has been completed through teamwork can bring.

'You look like a giant steaming turd.' Raspberry indicated Danny's filthy, drenched clothing. 'You'd have thought that with all this rain at least some of it might have washed off.'

'I know. Ellie will go spare. She hates mud anyway — and rain just as much. I'll have to strip stark bollock naked in the garden. She won't let me in the house like this.'

'Nor me. What is it with women and a little bit of mud? I love the stuff,' said Raspberry. 'And manure's even better.'

'It's a tad more than a little bit of mud, to be fair.'

'Well, they'd better get used to it. This is just the beginning. It still has to be spread and then dug in. It'll take all winter.'

He nodded towards one of the many huge piles of steaming dung that represented their day's labours.

'I'll never forget today,' said Raspberry. 'In the future, when we're as old as the Gaffer and Little Hands the Tomato Thief, we'll talk about how we used to be able to shift five tons of muck double-handed in the howling wind and pissing rain. Well, almost double-handed. Gaffer only had *two* barrowloads, Little Hands the Tomato Thief had *four* and Indian Ishaan had *seven*. It's all up here,' and he tapped his temple with his forefinger. 'But they're all still paying me a tenner each come what may. They can try and wriggle out of it as much as they like, the tight old bastards, but if they don't cough up I shall make their lives, or what's left of them, a bloody misery.'

'I'm giving up this lark,' said Danny. 'I'm forty-four you know and feel at least eighty-effing-eight. And one of my wellies is full of water. There's nothing worse than a wellie full of water.' With great difficulty he tugged it off, along with his sock, turned it over and poured a soupy stream, the colour of strong tea, onto the grass.

'You'll be here next year,' said Raspberry.

'You reckon? I wouldn't bank on it. I never want to shift another barrowload of shite ever again.'

'You've bugger all else to do and you'd miss me terribly.'

'I'd miss your Missus's strawberry jam terribly.'

'That's it though isn't it? If you work it out with labour and expenses and the cost of seeds, plant food, slug pellets, tools, getting ripped off by the Council for rent, getting ripped off by the Gaffer and his mates for manure, weedkiller, petrol for the rotavator and mower, canes, plant pots, compost, seed trays, then that pot of strawberry jam probably cost me twenty quid.'

'That's not really the way to look at it though. It's not about the money, it's about fresh air, job satisfaction, getting back to nature, fresh, uncontaminated food — they call it organic. There's a thousand and one things you get from an allotment.'

'Organic? What does that mean?'

'No pesticides.'

'No pesticides? Never heard anything so ridiculous in all my life. You need pesticides to get rid of — pests.'

'Well I never.'

'I smother my tack in it all the time. Good blast of Derris Dust does it the world of good. The Gaffer must've eaten tons of it in his time and look at him. He's perfectly preserved.'

'I rest my case.'

'Organic,' snorted Raspberry. 'Orgasmic more like, if Sid the Snail and his missus are anything to go by.'

'Ah, but Derris Dust could be a snail aphrodisiac which would account for the proliferation of the little bastards on your plot.'

'Good day though, wasn't it,' said Raspberry after a moment of deep reflection.

'I do admit to a certain sense of achievement despite being so shagged out I don't think I can walk home.'

'I'm soaked to the skin and starving. But it's a nice kind of soaked and starving, isn't it?' said Raspberry.

'What's the time?' asked Danny and with his arms spread wide and face lifted blissfully to the pouring rain, Raspberry sang back to him:

'It's a quarter to six and I know where we'll be,
Still shovelling shit in Sickletree.'

V / SEXT

MIDDAY PRAYER.

SIXTH HOUR.

APPROXIMATELY

12 NOON.

MATURITY

Christmas at Nazareth

UP AND DOWN THE lane they searched for what seemed like an age, asking for directions from kids, strangers, residents and even a cat but nobody had a clue where to find Mimosa Lodge. That was until an old man had pointed with his stick to a narrow drive between a wooden chalet bungalow and a cream cottage and told them that was where old Mrs So-and-So had lived, that she'd been there forever and that he didn't know it was up for sale and even if he did he wouldn't have bought it anyway because it was a cruddy dump. And it was only then that the house had offered up its secluded wonders. A walk up the aforementioned drive and through the holly-framed elmwood gate and they were in a brick-walled Victorian garden, completely sequestered from the world but in the hidden heart of old Sickletree and no more than a leisurely five-minute stroll from the shops and pubs in the Market Square. Just one look from the outside had told them that this place was perfect for their needs.

"Mimosa Lodge offers some roomy accommodation in a secluded area but is in need of much renovation and has been spoilt to some degree by surrounding development", read the jaundiced surveyor's report. Of this they took not one jot of notice.

Green Lane at that time was still bracketed by echoes of the countryside, despite being in the heart of the town. At one end was a working farm and at the other a plant nursery and the allotments. Of course, the house itself was shabby inside and out and in need of a lifetime of TLC but, once seen, all thoughts of moving to a box on one of the new estates was forgotten. The boys could safely ride their bikes around the garden paths, well away from the road and they could have a room each which, after the cramped confines of their previous home, was luxury living indeed.

They'd moved in just before Christmas and had sat exhausted on the timeworn parquet floor in front of a stuttering coal fire, surrounded by tea chests and later made the best of the festive season that they could. Danny came to believe that the house had been built for Christmas and looked forward to seeing the first frost on the hollies before the mistle thrushes moved in for their blood-red annual feast. Then there was the ivy which covered one of the garden walls and the sound of the band playing carols in the dark, snowy lane on their seasonal circuit of the town. Yes, the house was made for merrymaking in the heart of winter.

***

On the anniversary of their coming to Mimosa Lodge five years before, Danny was sitting in front of the TV and watching Scrooge go through his annual torture at the hands of the spirits. He arrived at this time every year jaded and bad tempered — perhaps they had taken on too much with the house after all, although every aspect of the Christmas celebrations always fell on Ellie. It was she that found the wreath for the door, she that shopped for the food, cooked it, put up the decorations, invited and looked after family and friends and generally saw to the thousand and one tasks that brought Christmas spirit into the home. All Danny could manage was to buy a box of cards and a few visits to the pub. There was no energy or interest in anything other than that token effort and he gradually came to despise the fake bonhomie and materialism of the time of year. Without knowing he had bought into Thatcher's Britain big time, was upwardly mobile and as miserable as sin. Christmas? Bah, humbug!

And there was good reason for that exhaustion. When he first saw the house Ellie's dad, Dimple, had laughed and said, 'But it's all fur coat and no drawers. You've some work on yer hands me boy.' And as a builder he knew what he was talking about. Over the long, sad years before they had arrived the sun had beaten down and parched the house, the rain had drowned it, the wind had battered it and the snow and frost had, bit by bit, devoured it.

But they had set about their monumental task with willing hearts and over the next few years Mimosa Lodge was insulated, damp-proofed, redecorated, rewired, replastered, refurnished, repointed and reroofed. It acquired a new bathroom, a new kitchen, new fireplaces, a new porch and a new garage. The coal hole was converted into a granny flat and absorbed into the house and pine cupboards purpose-built into the bedrooms and hall. The doors and stairs were stripped of paint and varnished and rotted windows and guttering were replaced. The exterior was repainted, garden walls were rebuilt and the courtyard garden landscaped and new lawns laid. The main garden had been lovingly restored by Ellie and honeysuckle and clematis grew in the place of vine, bracken and weeds. Crumbling chimney stacks had been rebuilt, the summer house demolished and central heating installed. Now the old lady stood in the winter sunshine as attractive and desirable as she had been when built over a hundred years before. But this miraculous return to her youth had come at a heavy price. Add to this the demands of a growing family, whilst holding down the day jobs and Ellie and Danny were at the end of their energies. Ellie bore her exhaustion with patience and calm but Danny's mid-life crisis was a different matter. He had pushed himself to the limit in every direction and all work and no play had made Jack a very unhappy boy.

The doorbell rang and a disgruntled Danny heaved himself away from Ebenezer and his tormentors. A Pickwickian figure on the doorstep, rotund and small, beamed at him through a sparse black goatee. He could have been any age between twenty-five and fifty.

'Who is it?' shouted Ellie from the kitchen.

'Bob Scratchit,' shouted Danny.

'What does he want?'

'What do you want, O'Mara?'

'And a festive Yuletide greetings of the seasonal variety to you as well, Mr Scrooge,' said the bearer of tidings of comfort and joy. 'Can I speak to Ellie?'

'Wait here a minute,' said Danny and he walked through to the kitchen.

'Who is it?' whispered Ellie.

'It's bloody O'Mara again and at just the wrong time as usual,' said Danny petulantly.

'Well, let him in then, Scrooge. It's bitter out there.'

'Do I have to? I was hoping for some peace and quiet today.'

'I know, but you can't leave one of my friends out there. Let him in at —'

'I like this house,' said O'Mara as he strode uninvited into the kitchen. 'You're always guaranteed a warm welcome here.' He radiated bonhomie and sarcasm in equal measure.

'Cuppa tea, Treacle?' asked Ellie.

'Wouldn't say no to a cuppa *and* a bacon sandwich, seeing as you're offering. I have been told I am looking anorexic,' said O'Mara as he slapped his bulging abdomen.

'And I think a few of the seasonal mince pies and a large slice of the excellent Crimble cake you buy at enormous expense from the Samuel Pepys Tea Rooms each Yuletide would also be appropriate, don't you, Treacle?' he added.

'That can be arranged for a person as elevated as your good self,' said Ellie, remembering he was now, "Councillor O'Mara".

'If the pair of you are going to talk about your good works for the community them I'm off into the other room,' said Danny.

'Farewell then, Mr Scrooge,' said O'Mara. 'Have an extremely droll Christmas and a miserable New Year.'

'Before I go can you tell me why you both call each other Treacle? It sounds a bit daft for grown ups don't you think?'

O'Mara and Ellie looked at each other and laughed.

Quite what irritated Danny most about O'Mara, wasn't clear. Was it his good heart or the fact that he had never bought into the system that was slowly destroying Danny? He lived in a trailer on a farm in the middle of nowhere in some sort of hippy commune whilst Danny himself had lost that brand of idealism years before. It had been eroded by the grindstone of what he saw as the multitude of life's realities such as paying bills and putting food on the table. 'Surely there's more to life than this?' he asked himself. That there could be another way to live irked Danny immensely as it made all of his unhappiness so unnecessary and threw a spotlight on his blossoming materialism and conformity.

Yes, that was it. O'Mara would not be bought by the system and lived his life as a free man, unbound by the trappings of the modern age and Danny was jealous of O'Mara's freedom and happiness and had himself become a sad and grey man.

'What did Bob Scratchit want in the end?' asked Danny sulkily after the little man had gone. 'And why does he think it's okay to swan in like he owns the place?'

'That,' said Ellie and she indicated a cheap Christmas card whose glitter had showered the kitchen worktop with a drift of tacky diamond dust.

Danny opened it and read aloud.

As you are both not "normal" and therefore definitely one of us, you are both cordially invited to our Festive Extravaganza at Nazareth Farm on Christmas Eve. Please bring a bottle, an odd sense of humour and a bucket — you're going to need them!
O'Mara and the Elves

'So, a Christmas party at Nazareth. How appropriate and just what we need to lift our spirits,' said Ellie.

'Speak for yourself,' said Scrooge.

(THE BELL RINGS FOR SEXT)

The first serious frost of winter had dallied well into the morning as they slowly drove the serpentine road out from Sickletree to Nazareth Farm. A vivid sun, low in a watercolour wash sky shone unblinking through the windscreen making driving a matter of guesswork and Danny tutted and moaned at every shuddering jolt from the pothole-strewn tarmac.

'"I pulled into Nazareth, was feelin' about half past dead". Who sang that? What album is it off and it was also released as a single but in what year?'

'The Band,' she answered. 'It's off the *Music from Big Pink* album. And it was released as a single in sixty-eight, I believe. I had just started at college.'

'And your final question is, what is the song called?'

'It's called "The Weight".'

'Congratulations. You have won first prize, which is spending Christmas Eve with a bunch of weirdos who live in squalor in the back of beyond.'

'Don't be like that, it's very kind of them to ask us.'

'They asked you, not me. Tell me why they'd want Scrooge humbugging away at their Christmas party.'

'Well, think of it as an offer of redemption, such as you were granted in *A Christmas Carol*.'

'Well, seeing that O'Mara's now on the Town Council maybe he could do something about the mess the road out to his place is in. You know, at least try and bring it up to third world standard. It's like driving around Beirut.'

'Mind that pot —' The car slumped into a hole that felt as deep and wide as a bomb crater and muddy water sloshed the screen.

'I can't see,' said Danny. 'I'm going to have to stop for a while.'

They waited until the sun finally began to dip behind the hills and it was with the gift of restored eyesight that they found the dirt track that led off the lane and up to the farm.

'What are those?' asked Danny pointing to a group of black silhouettes in a field.

'They're buffaloes. The farmer that rents the land makes mozzarella from their milk.'

'Weird or what? I'm not looking forward to this one bit.'

They found O'Mara still asleep in his foetid pink and mould-mottled mobile home. With some difficulty they woke him by banging a heavy stick on the flaking door.

'Welcome to the Turdis, headquarters of the Nazareth Crimble Festivities. Fancy a bacon sandwich to line the old bread basket before the forthcoming indulgences, Treacle and Ebenezer?' he asked the pair.

'No thanks,' said Danny after checking the frying pan.

'You're missing a festive treat,' he said as he yawned and scratched his ample backside.

'So this is where you live, O'Mara,' said Danny eyeing the squalid accommodation sardonically. 'I always said you'd make good trailer trash.'

O'Mara fell out of bed, threw a heap of rashers and eggs into the blackened pan and began his fry-up in his ragged underwear. The grease looked as if it hadn't been changed for at least a year. He brewed some equally suspicious looking tea for the visitors which Danny deliberately let go cold after he noticed the scum on the surface of the brew and the stains around the lip of the cup.

'Bit of a hygiene issue here isn't there, O'Mara?'

'Just you wait 'til you see the main course — roast goose with all the trimmings. The bird is being cooked over a paraffin fire as we speak.'

'Paraffin? You *are* joking me?'

'We are full of innovative culinary ideas at Nazareth.'

After his meal, O'Mara threw on an Iron Maiden t-shirt, candy-striped shorts and a vintage dragon-patterned silk kimono dressing gown. On his sockless feet he wore his "slippers" — a pair of old woman's ankle boots, lined with fake fur and still caked with the dried manure that had covered them when they were left unclaimed after a Baptist church tombola. A Rupert Bear

TAROT

scarf, wrapped around his head toothache style, completed the outfit. This was his improvised Christmas party attire and he wore it for the rest of the night. He guided the visitors across the derelict farmyard to a tiny caravan that had been forsaken countless years before and left to disintegrate in a large oily puddle.

'Before we start, I have a special treat for you. You have a special invitation to meet the world-renowned Gypsy Rose Futt, in the luxury of the Vomit Wagon.' O'Mara banged heavily on the flimsy caravan with a clenched fist and stepped back.

'Patience, are you in there, you dotty old bag?' he screamed at the door after a long silence.

'Who the *fuck* is it?' demanded an ethereal female voice.

'Well, who the fuck do you *think* it is — Patrick Swayze?'

After a second or two the door flew open and a woman's hand, festooned with bangles, rings and occult charms, poked a smoking reefer through a beaded curtain that concealed the interior.

'Smoke this before you come in — you need to have the correct vibrations,' ordered the disembodied voice. 'I'm seeing to the bird.' The smell of paraffin and burning feathers wafted from the caravan and even overpowered the weed. So O'Mara hadn't been joking about the gastronomical procedures at Nazareth.

O'Mara offered the joint to Danny and Ellie but they both declined. O'Mara shrugged, took a couple of disinterested puffs, coughed violently and flicked the stub into a puddle.

'Finished,' he shouted to the Vomit Wagon. 'We are now in tune with the cosmos, Oh, Enlightened One. Can I rescue the bird please. I think it's best either cooked whole over the bonfire or in sections on the barbecue rather than over a paraffin stove. Not very normal, paraffin as a cooking fuel. Not very Egon Ronay.'

There was a long pause before a steaming and badly plucked goose was fed with some difficulty through the beads.

'Do with it as you see fit,' said the disembodied voice. 'I don't wish to see the bloody thing again until it is on my plate, smothered in apple-cider gravy and chestnut stuffing.'

O'Mara disappeared into the dark carrying the smoking bird.

'Come and help me with the cooking, Treacle — it's only Danny that Patience wants to read anyway.' And in a second Danny was on his own.

'Enter,' said the voice. Danny parted the bead curtains and peered into the darkened interior. A few charred goose feathers smoked on the floor and the heat inside was overpowering. As his eyes became accustomed to the gloom he spotted at the far end of the van a stout woman of about fifty wearing the sourest of expressions. She was sitting next to an ancient paraffin stove which was releasing a thin, black, oily trail of smoke from its mesh flame cover. Her long red hair had been tied back with a yellow bandana and her gaudy make-up had been clumsily applied — so badly in fact that her crimson lipstick covered most of her face and her smudged mascara made her eyes look like coals.

'Greetings, I am Patience, the wife of Adam Futt, the owner of Nazareth Farm. Come over here and sit please. I assume that you want a reading?' She looked at Danny as if he were dirt.

'Er, no. I don't believe in —'

Patience ignored him and produced a pack of tarot cards. She frowned and began obsessively dealing the cards in perfect lines, face up on to a paint-splattered Black & Decker Workmate.

'The Hanged Man — the sitter possesses an extremely mean streak with money.

'Oh dear, The Hermit — you are lonely, isolated, and have lost your way.'

A black cat with enormous eyes sneaked into the warmth and rubbed itself sinuously against Danny's leg. It miaowed plaintively.

'Quiet please, Beelzebub. Mother is busy.'

Patience turned another card.

'The Chariot — lack of control and direction, aggressive.

'The Emperor — you're tyrannical, weak and cold.

'The Fool — reckless and inconsiderate.

'The Star — faithless and insecure.'

She paused and pushed a black cigarette into an ivory holder.

'This is quite the worst reading I've ever given.' She gave Danny a piercing stare of undisguised disgust as she concluded her negative stream of consciousness.

'I think there's a strong possibility you may have mistaken me for someone else,' said Danny. 'None of that is me.'

Patience wrapped her arms around her ample bosom, closed her eyes and began humming to herself as she rocked to and fro. At one point Danny thought she was about to fall off her chair. Even the cat looked alarmed.

'No, it is *you*, Danny, husband of Ellie, also known as the Mizzog of Sickletree, who stands before me and whose fortune has been revealed by the cards,' she intoned in an otherworldly voice. 'Hmmaaooh,' she moaned as if in torment.

'Well, it's not so much a fortune, is it? More like a character assassination, to be fair.'

The inaccurately named Patience angrily snapped out of her trance and gave a brutal summing up. Danny was a guilt-stricken control freak, an angry and active misogynist, an animal-hating homophobe and a psychopath who suffered from a repressed Oedipus complex. It was all in the cards.

Well, that's the full deck, thought Danny and I've got a very good idea who's behind this and they're not very far from here, hopefully making themselves useful by rescuing a charred goose from a culinary fate worse than death.

Her work done, Patience gave him a ghastly smile and held out a hand. Danny shook it but she coughed expectantly and the hand remained in place. Now, realising what was expected of him, Danny thanked her politely and crossed her palm with silver (a twenty-pence piece), mumbled his excuses and then walked off towards the halo and hubbub of the silhouetted farmhouse, trailed by Beelzebub who, attracted by the smell of incinerated goose, followed him like a long lost friend.

***

To escape the cold a theatre of shadow puppets had gathered around the runaway bonfire as it spangled the winter night with skybound sparklers of red, orange and gold. Over the nearby Windrush a wolf moon studied its rippling reflection with an impassive gaze until the river's secret murmurings were disturbed by the percussive bang of an arbitrary firework. The boom was saluted by a ragged cheer from within the fiery circle of celebration.

They sang carols to the accompaniment of an out-of-tune four-string guitar, pulled charred chestnuts from the edge of the fire and threw them from hand to hand until cool. They ate slabs of home-made, filling-puller toffee, crunched sweet apples until the juice ran down their chins and cracked hazelnuts with stones. They ate poached pears in syrup, treacle tart and mince pies with fresh buffalo cream and cinnamon buns dripping with butter, honey and cherry jam. They drank nettle beer and home-made lemonade, raisin wine, sloe gin and a ferociously spiced rum punch. And all the while, O'Mara, in his bizarre outfit, was the glue that quietly coalesced the evening, moving from person to person and effortlessly blending the various groups into a whole. From time to time he disappeared into the night to "check the bird".

Danny got caught in the moment and lost track of time. He made new friends of people that in normal circumstances he could have easily dismissed, listened instead of boasting and felt the freedom to engage at a much deeper level than was admissible in his business life. He met Teacup and his wife Lily, Josh and his wife Em, Adam and Patience's kids, Adam Junior and Eve, Pedro, Tappy, Baz, Baggs, Buddy and his wife Maude — Bohemians to a man, woman and child. He found to his surprise that night that he had a much deeper care and interest in the lives of others than was customary for him and rapidly became drunk on the elusive spirit of Christmas as it poured into his abstemious heart. As a man reborn he reflected that he hadn't so much as sniffed the reefer that Patience had materialised through the Vomit Wagon's door. Something soft wrap itself around his legs. It was Beelzebub. Even the pets welcomed him at Nazareth.

'Esteemed and beloved guests,' boomed a tall figure in druidic robes and garlanded in mistletoe. 'I am Amergin and I welcome you to Earthworm Hall to celebrate the winter solstice.'

The doors of a decrepit barn were flung wide open and the revellers followed Amergin into a radiant candlelit space where shadows boogied behind a magnificent hammerbeam ceiling and beautifully crafted decorations of holly, mistletoe and ivy had been hung from the walls and beams. A scratchy fanfare of trumpets greeted the parade as it strode at a regal pace into the barn and past an imposing Yuletide tableau which featured a manger made from a wooden palette with "Welcome to Nazareth!" stencilled in stark black lettering on the front. Inside was a china girl-doll which had been swaddled in a tea towel and covered in straw — an unlit cheroot was in its mouth. The happy parents were shop mannequins; Mary was dressed in a stained quilt cover and was missing an arm; Joseph was trouserless in a donkey jacket but with his modesty thoughtfully protected by a pair of paisley boxer shorts. To one side a donkey, or possibly a reindeer, had been hastily built from bamboo canes and was feeding from a box of sawdust with a lugubrious expression. Three newspaper crowns represented the Magi who had obviously seen enough and gone home.

Amergin, who turned out to be Adam Futt, sat at the head of the table, beaming, waving and holding hands with Patience, benevolent and silent apart from proposing the occasional toast.

Danny approached the meal with trepidation. He had already noticed that hygiene on the farm was nothing more than basic and had carefully avoided anything so far that appeared suspect, which included everything apart from an apple and some nuts. But by now he was starving and decided to take the risk. The goose tasted of bonfire with a slight chemical aftertaste but he decided that it was his imagination and that it was edible. The trimmings were mountainous bowls of emerald sprouts sprinkled with diced roast chestnuts, peas in shredded coconut, honey-glazed carrots and parsnips and towering jugs of gravy. Finally, a blazing Christmas pudding the width of a dustbin lid, was trundled into the barn in a wheelbarrow and rapidly went the same way as the goose.

'Enjoying it, Treacle?' O'Mara asked Ellie. 'This is my third Christmas dinner so far this week. Everyone I visit wants me to help with the cooking and then join in after. Be rude not to.'

There was a short interlude in the eating where O'Mara handed out presents, which had been wrapped in copies of *The Sun*, to the over-excited kids.

'O'Mara, you lovely man,' said Patience theatrically after she had received her present. 'If you weren't my tenant I'd definitely —' and she smothered him in kisses.

A sprout whizzed past Danny's ear followed by a half-chewed parsnip. Oh no, not a food fight — this really vexed his puritanical streak. In no time the leftovers covered the people and the floor of the barn and sprouts dribbled down the walls like a scene from a nineteen-fifties goo-flick.

'It's The Blob,' shouted O'Mara in mock terror at a luminous green splodge as it bubbled on the floor. 'But are *you* eating *it*, or is *it* eating *you*? Beware of radioactive brassicas.'

Danny resolved his unease by deciding that the food wasn't being wasted — throwing it around let off some high spirits and was better than throwing insults. Although he'd often been hungry in his early life he could definitely live with wasting sprouts.

'I want to be an entrepreneur and one day I'll have a home and family like yours,' offered O'Mara out of the blue.

The three of them were back in the Turdis having quit the mayhem after saying goodnight. O'Mara had acquired a pair of reindeer horns during the evening which lit up intermittently and his lips were smudged with rouge and lipstick where he'd been over-kissed by an emotional Patience. His kimono was open at the stomach revealing a hairy navel set in a beachball bubble of flesh. He took a long reflective pull from his bottle of home-made sloe gin. Neither Danny or Ellie had seen him this drunk before.

'Believe you me, O'Mara, you're better of in your trailer. What you lose is greater than what you gain when you start on that path,' said Danny. 'You're speaking to someone who knows.'

'Don't say that in front of Treacle — you wouldn't change your situation for the world. You just need to change your mindset.'

'And you wouldn't change your mindset for the world, just your situation,' laughed Danny. 'People, eh? Always wanting what they haven't got.'

'But of all things it's the people who are not normal. Nothing about them makes any sense. Not normal, that's my view of most of the people in this world.'

'Talking of not being normal, do please tell me you two were behind that seance shit with Patience. I'm not really like that am I? I mean, it was all so negative.'

'The cards do not lie,' said O'Mara.

'Would it really matter either way? I'm sure what she told you was the truth,' said Ellie, stage-winking at O'Mara.

'Here's something for you,' said O'Mara.

He handed Danny an object which had been hastily wrapped in plain brown paper and stuck with duck tape. It had "For Mr Scrooge" written on it in smudged felt pen.

'I found it in a car boot sale. It cost twenty-five pence, so no expense spared for a friend. You need some sunshine in your life and so it made me think of you. It's a Zen candle-holder, made in the depths of darkest Brummagem. So when things get tough, get it out and remember to lighten up yourself as well as the candle and think of me as you do.'

'I'll stick it in the bog then. I haven't anything for you, O'Mara, but then what do you get the man who has everything?'

'No worries at all. Just make Treacle here and the boys happy. That'll do for me.'

'I see you now for who you are, O'Mara. You are none other than the Ghost of Christmas Present.'

'You have to be lots of things to your family: breadwinner, defender, lover, hero and psychiatrist but the most important is to be the one who brings some sunshine into their lives. Nothing else really matters apart from that, does it? I'm not sure I could be that person and that's why I've never tried.'

'You'd be a great dad, O'Mara,' said Ellie.

'Well, we'll never know will we.'

Danny looked at his watch.

'God, is it that time?' said Ellie. 'We'd better go. Granny Esther has got the boys and we said we'd be back by ten.'

'Merry Christmas you two and remember to light a candle for me,' said O'Mara as he waved goodbye from the Turdis door.

'A great day, Treacle,' said Ellie and she gave him a smacker on the cheek. 'We *have* got you something — it's in the car.'

'Thanks, Treacle. I really do hope it's not a portable computer — we haven't got electricity at Nazareth,' said O'Mara with a deadpan face.

***

'Now *that's* what Christmas is all about,' said Danny as, guided by a single bright star on the eastern horizon, he drove slowly home.

'Did you enjoy your evening?'

'Not so much *enjoy* as *learnt* something.'

'Which was?'

'Not to eat a goose that's been cooked in paraffin. I think I may have the stirrings of Delhi belly.'

'No, seriously.'

'I was being serious.'

'Well, in that case you'd better sleep on the sofa.'

'I would say that today I learnt that Christmas is not about what you are given or even what you give but about paying closer attention to what you already have. I don't think I've met so many people who have different ways of living their lives from mine and yet I liked pretty much all of them. Nobody preached and everyone was accepted with understanding and patience. Even a well-known misery like me.'

'It sounds like today was time well spent after all.'

'Oh, and another thing I learnt is to stop being so judgemental. Cut people some slack. We're all in the same boat after all.'

Ellie nodded. 'We're all just walking each other home.'

They drove on in silence until the car hit a pothole concealed from the weak headlights by the darkness of the road.

'Did you tell Councillor O'Mara his road needs fixing?'

'I did.'

'Well, what did he say?'

'In a nutshell he told me it was nothing to do with him and to get stuffed.'

'I see.'

'But he said it in a nice way.'

'Treat others as you wish to be treated. You can still tell people what you think without being nasty,' said Danny.

'Sometimes life throws lessons at you all at once. They come thick and fast.'

'Blimey, I think I'd better start taking notes,' said Danny. 'I'm sure I'm going to forget all of this when I get back to work.'

As they pulled up outside of No 12, they saw Granny Esther framed in the window, holding the youngest boy close to her chest and she waved his little hand as she saw them get out of the car.

'Lucky aren't we?' said Danny.

'Very.'

'I need to remember that and not just at Christmas. Every day.'

'I'll remind you if you like,' said Ellie and she pretended to wallop his backside like a naughty boy as she chased him up the drive and into the house.

VI / NONE

MID-AFTERNOON

PRAYER.

NINTH HOUR.

APPROXIMATELY 3PM.

OLD AGE

The Angel Investor

NEANDER WOKE EARLY FROM a bad dream. He had been working in a bleak office which was trapped within a soulless building in the centre of a dreary city. It was a Friday and he had left work early to go home but couldn't remember where he'd left his car. He wandered the filthy streets for what seemed like hours as a dreadful night fell but he had no memory of where he'd left his only means of escape from this terrible place. He stepped over rows of the homeless, sleeping in their cardboard shacks, snuggled in their filthy sleeping bags. After a while even the destitute had departed, leaving the streets empty apart from the windswept litter and Alexander Neander's lost, wandering soul. It was just as he spied three threatening silhouettes step out of an alleyway and begin to follow him that he gratefully awoke from his nightmare. His sparse bedroom with its floral wallpaper in his tiny bungalow on the outskirts of Sickletree seemed almost welcoming. A dismal feeling of despair brought on by the dream lingered doggedly and left a gloom that even his habitually frugal breakfast of toast and jam could not dispel.

He checked himself in the bathroom mirror and ruffled his hair — the frizz of gunmetal grey released drifts of dandruff on to the narrow shoulders of his threadbare suit. Neander had recently lost a front tooth which, after some deliberation, he had decided against getting fixed as it reminded him of that callous thief, time: forever changing, forever meddling, forever taking. It was not as if the world was to know anyway, as he never smiled in public. Or private for that matter. Instead he left the gap as another of his special secrets, only to be revealed after his death.

When these moods took him, as they did more frequently nowadays, Neander would spend a little time in the triangular red-brick museum situated where the road forked on the Oxford Road on his walk to work. The old town in the photo display had faded like a ghost in a summer twilight. Walrus Toys had become an estate agent, the fishmonger was now an antique shop and the butcher, with its grisly display of hanging pheasants and executed rabbits, was empty and had been for years. Booth's Emporium was now an expensive delicatessen and the men's outfitters had become a pretentious restaurant that nobody, including even the town's upper echelons, could possibly afford to patronise. The Wonky Donkey was still there of course (pubs at least appeared to be everlasting) albeit with a clumsy new sign and the Warwickshire Yeomanry, pictured in high spirits in the Market Square with their horses and a howitzer en route to France in the summer of 1914, had left for destruction at the front, well over sixty-years before. No Badger's Nest café — that was now a building society, no Baptist chapel which had transmogrified into unaffordable luxury apartments and Wass & Wass Ironmongers was extinct — another charity shop. There was the legendary Sickletree Excelsior

12
1
2
3
4
5
6
7
8
9
10
11

football team parading the 1931 Hospital Cup in their huge shorts and unfashionable hoops. "Captain Nobby Berry holds the trophy aloft with a resounding 'hurrah' from his splendid team and its supporters". Whole rows of smoking terraced houses in Paradise Lane, The Bury and Britannia Way had disappeared under time's remorseless scythe. Cars now clogged the pavements of those once empty streets, where easily contented children had innocently played and where the majestic shire horse had stepped proudly out into the morning of the world. And it was all so unnecessarily and utterly sad, thought the cadaverous man as he scratched his brillo pad hair and released yet more dandruff on to a display case that held an assortment of broken clay pipes. A lot of these people and places he remembered first-hand and he had become a silent witness to their creeping destruction and a guardian of their memory. What had been lost was irreplaceable.

He went back to the photo of the Warwickshire Yeomanry and huffed and polished the lenses of his heavy-framed tortoiseshell glasses. With a single crooked forefinger he wiped the side of his eagle's beak of a nose and he studied the image more intimately. At the front of the crowded throng of excited men he picked out an adolescent soldier, seated on a kerb with a plume of blurred smoke escaping his laughing mouth. He stood out from his mates because he was the only soldier who was bareheaded and without a moustache. He was looking directly at Neander who had taken the place of the unknown photographer behind the primitive box camera. Another of time's strange miracles. For a brief moment there was a silent intimacy between the two. So far away and yet so close. I wonder who you were, he thought. What was your name? How did it end for you? Did you stay happy? What was your story? Outside, the heavy traffic thundered past and drenched the museum's faux gothic windows with muddy rainwater.

***

Neander worked alone to the somnolent accompaniment of clocks — a hundred sets of footsteps, all marching forward, but all out of time. He could identify each one by their tick or tock. They were like people — every one had a personality, each one a voice. He loved their music; it was an orchestra to him. And he loved time as well, though he found its destructive tendencies terrifying. All of those people and most of the places he had seen in the photographs in the museum had been destroyed in a million different ways by time. He had read somewhere that those fools of eastern philosophers said that time didn't exist and that life was a dream, but he knew in his bitter heart they were all wrong. What did they know? He worked with time, was surrounded by it every second of his day and he loved it like a mistress. That was why he worshipped the past — time was inscribed in the rock of ages. He kept a secret collection of devil's toenails, the fossilised shells of sea creatures that he regularly uncovered in his garden, as rock-solid proof as to the power, majesty and existence of time. If he could live in the past he would. Things were more ordered then, people were stronger, wiser, calmer, kinder and happier. Yes, it was much better then. He had not called his business in Cider Mill Lane, Precious Time without a reason. Time was precious they said. Now that *was* right. Time was precious and that was why he was so mean with it and why he refused to share it with anyone. The saddest thing in the world was to hear some poor fool say they never had any time. That was poverty indeed. If someone wasted Neander's time it was like stealing his money, so he never gave it away with good reason. It was said that the only two things of value in life are time and love and you can't live without either. Alexander Neander disagreed. He could live without love.

(THE BELL RINGS FOR NONE)

The clocks were striking three as the brass doorbell clanged and added to the din. Neander looked up from the heart of a priceless Whitehurst where he had been totally absorbed by the intricate machinery that laid bare the thoughts of a man who had been dead for nearly two hundred years. Though he hardly noticed the chimes, the doorbell he definitely did and it irked him.

'Can I help you,' he asked of a diminutive man of late middle-age in a manner that indicated that he meant the exact opposite. What irritated him more than being interrupted from his work was that there was something familiar about the man which Neander couldn't place.

'Maybe,' responded the visitor confidently. 'I don't know if you remember me but I worked here when you bought this place — when it was called The Sickletree Hours. You said you couldn't afford to keep me on so I had to leave. I don't know if you know but Mr Shuckleberry died not long after. Very sad. After I left here all those years ago, I had what I suppose you'd now call a breakdown. My mechanism ran out of spring as it were. I was only young and didn't think anybody would want me as I had so little experience. Obviously, the family were young as well and they depended on me so much that I felt I'd let them down. But I had to find the strength to pick myself up and find some belief from somewhere. We decided to move away from Sickletree and make a new start.'

Neander had hoped that all the visitor wanted was a watch battery and would be on his way in no time but this candid and unsolicited disclosure was the last thing he needed today or any other day for that matter.

'Yes, I vaguely remember you now. What can I do for you?'

'Ah, a Whitehurst,' said the visitor. 'A wonderful clock and one of my all-time favourites.'

'Quite,' said Neander. 'An interesting story you tell, but I'm not sure what it has to do with me Mr —?'

'Here's my card. I own the Pendulum franchise of clock shops. The name's Faith. Clarence Faith. You are Mr Alexander Neander aren't you — if I remember correctly?'

'Yes,' said Neander tetchily. 'You seem to know quite a lot about me.'

'Well, as I said, I've been through a bad time myself — very similar to the one you're going through now — so I wondered if you needed a change of direction in life and would agree to sell Precious Time to me? I'll give you a good price.'

'Huh? Sell?' said Neander menacingly. 'Sell? Now, tell me why on earth would I want to do that? And what do you mean about me having a bad time? My life is no business of yours.' This innocuous little man had instantly got under his skin.

Neander fell silent as the doorbell clanged once more and a very old lady with a Zimmer frame walked haltingly up to the counter. The men watched her struggle in silence.

'Ah, Mrs Pettifoot,' said Neander. 'I'm afraid your Whitehurst is not ready. I've been very busy and had a lot of distractions lately.' He looked pointedly at Faith. 'Would you be so kind as to come back in a couple of days, Madam, and I should be finished. Thank you so very much,' and he dismissed her with an imperious wave.

There was an awkward silence before the door closed with a clang and the pair resumed their fraught discussion.

'Look, as you see, I need to get on,' said Neander eager to terminate the conversation. He indicated the open heart of the Whitehurst on his workbench. 'Major surgery needed and time waits for no man. You know how it is.'

'Yes, I understand,' said the visitor and he turned to go.

'It's just to say that if you ever reconsider then do please get in touch. And please will you keep my card on file?'

'Yes, Mr Faith, of course,' said Neander, happy that things appeared to be drawing to a conclusion.

'It could be if things continue to be bad that you might find the belief that your life can improve. It was my faith that got me through — Faith by name, faithful by nature. A belief in better times ahead is sometimes all you need.'

Neander didn't trust himself to continue the dialogue. He turned his back on the man, walked back to his workbench and pretended to dissect the Whitehurst until he heard the doorbell jangle. He didn't realise he had been holding his breath until he let out the air in a rush of relief.

The clockmaker was more shaken by his recent visitor than he cared to admit and couldn't concentrate on the Whitehurst despite the task being so complicated that it needed his undivided attention. He stopped for a short tea break which helped him to recover his equilibrium somewhat but he still obsessively mulled over the encounter. Who the hell did that peculiar man think he was? An almost total stranger who wandered in off the street, tried to convince him what a rotten life he's having and then casually offers to buy his lifetime's work as if he was doing Neander a favour. Was it that he still bore a grudge and wanted to let Neander know about his success? If so, why bother? Neander couldn't care less about the silly little man and his feeble machinations. Just let him bother Neander again with his half-baked business propositions and amateur psychoanalysis sessions and see where that got him.

He lifted his head from working on the clock, stretched his back with a groan and nearly jumped out of his skin. How on earth had that woman got into the shop without him hearing the doorbell? Maybe she came in when Faith left? She looked at him silently; her pale face carried a haunted and concerned look.

'Hope?'

'I'm sorry, Alexander, I didn't mean to startle you.'

'Well, you certainly did. I mean what are you *doing* here? After all this time.'

She said nothing but placed a small, blue box on the polished walnut counter between them.

'What's this?'

'You gave this present to me years ago when we were together. Remember? Well, I want you to have it back. And the reason for that is I haven't got much time.'

Neander knew only too well what an unforgiving miser time could be. Time never gave more than it could afford. None of us had too much time.

'What do you mean?'

'What I say. I'm dying.'

'You can't be.' By questioning the truth Neander had given himself a brief opportunity to avoid it but he realised too late how stupid his response had been. All of us were dying thanks to time.

Hope nodded towards the box. 'You said at the time that it's a gift that will last a lifetime. Well mine is nearly over so I'm giving it back to you as, by living, you will have more need of it than me.'

'Hope, it needn't have been like this.'

'Does it matter? You made a choice and acted upon it.'

'Why have you come to me? I can't give you any more time than you already have,' he pleaded as he indicated the myriad of clocks that covered the walls of the shop. 'I have the method of marking time but not the means to give it,' he added in desperation. 'I just help measure the grinding machinery of life.'

'Perhaps if you lived in the moment rather than the past it might be easier to understand.'

'Understand what?'

'Love.'

'Love?'

'Yes, love. Instead of constantly mulling over things, why don't you just let them happen. You were never able to do that. Everything had to be controlled from the safety of the past — from the knowledge of experience.'

'I genuinely don't know what you mean or how I can help you. Everything between us ended many years ago. If you've come to say goodbye, then say it and go. I'm sorry about your sad news but there's nothing more left to say or anything I can do. Now, if you don't mind, I'm busy —'

'Okay, Alexander, I will go now. I had hoped for a different response but do enjoy the gift,' she said indicating the box again. 'I'm sure it'll fetch a good price,' she added bitterly and with that she was gone.

Neander stood there, too shocked at her sudden departure to speak. After a while he picked up the box and opened it. Inside was a beautifully crafted Faith, Hope and Charity silver necklace. He studied it minutely with a professional eye and read the exquisitely engraved inscription he had written a lifetime before.

Be Bold, Be Strong In Times Of Change.
Forever Yours — Alexander

What was happening today? First that odd businessman and now an ex-lover come to say that she was at the end. He didn't have enough time left himself to waste it on shilly-shalliers, no matter their current situation or past relationship to him. Living in the past wasn't about being controlled by its inhabitants. He felt like putting up the closed sign and shutting up shop for what was left of the afternoon but apart from a handful of browsers and those two unwanted visitors, he had hardly seen a soul all day and the leasehold still had to be paid. After thoughtfully tossing the blue box between shaking hands he put it in his briefcase and gratefully returned to the Whitehurst to help him make sense of the day.

***

Neander was just about to finish his work. He had decided to follow his instinct to shut up early and had turned off the paraffin stove and compulsively packed his tools away in the correct drawers of his antique tool box. His old boss, Mr Gastrell of Stratford-upon-Avon, had told him — "always pack up the night before and save yourself time the following morning". He loved that concept — a solid investment in time that bought financial rewards. Time now for a takeaway curry from the Bengali, a glass of wine and an early night to help him put this strange day behind him.

'Are you the owner?' A ragged figure shouted through the glass just as he was about to put up the closed sign and she pushed the door wide open, knocking him backwards in surprise. The rain was still coming down in sheets and she was soaked to the skin.

'We're closed, Madam,' said Neander unbelievingly.

A young girl, probably still a teenager, with heavily tattooed arms and neck stared straight back at him. Her purple hair hung in damp knots and she had piercings in her nose, cheek and lip. She wiped the diluted snot from her upper lip onto her sleeve.

'You can find the charity shops in the Market Square,' said Neander dismissively. 'And I was just about to close when you pushed your way in.'

'I don't need charity. What I need is a job. Please,' she added as an afterthought.

'Well it would be charity,' said Neander. 'You're of absolutely no use to me whatsoever.' Would you believe yet another bloody timewaster. Do they always come in groups of three? he asked himself. Why was everybody demanding something of him today?

He had a realisation. 'Your name wouldn't be Charity by any chance would it?'

'No it's Gift. Amelia Gift.'

'Hmm,' said Neander, not convinced. First Faith, then Hope —

'Please hear me out, ' said the girl. 'Just give me five minutes of your time.'

'I don't have five minutes to give,' said Neander. Yet another chancer wanting his precious time free of charge.

The girl ignored him and persevered.

'I studied engineering at uni and was doing well until my third year when my mum suddenly died. After that I just gave up and dropped out. She was all I had and I struggled like mad without her guidance. I'll not hide it — I have drug and drink issues and nowhere to live at the moment. But I have a deep interest in clocks. Well, actually, I have a deep interest in *time*. That would be closer to the truth. My mum left me a beautiful grandfather clock. It's all I have left to remember her by. On the face it says, "Time is the wisest counsellor of all" — Pericles, I think.'

'Well you've hardly given me a glowing curriculum vitae in order to boost your prospects have you?'

'I'm just being honest. And with that honesty and desperation comes a need that will see me work as hard as I can. I can clean, make tea, help with the books, answer the phone, take orders — anything. All you have to do in return is pay me a basic wage and teach me all that you know.'

'All that I know? Well, there's a pretty thing. All that I know, eh? And what makes you think I have a spare forty years or so to waste while you struggle to get yourself off the drink and drugs?'

'You won't be able to tell what I'm capable of until you've given me a chance. All I ask for is a trial opportunity. A month at the most. I won't let you down.'

'And what's in it for me then, Miss Gift? I would have to waste so much of my time in teaching you, that I would need to have a very good reason to become your angel investor.'

'Your reward would be knowing that your knowledge would live on after you've gone. I'd carry on your work so that all of your time spent at that bench hasn't been wasted.'

This hit Neander like a hammer blow to the head. So that his time would not have been wasted, she had said. Oh my God, perish the thought. He'd never thought of it like that before. All this will die with him. What a clever girl. Whether by fortune or design she'd instantly found his Achilles heel.

'My time has *not* been wasted young lady. I don't waste one *minute* of it, I can assure you and have *never* done so. During the whole of my sixty-seven years on this earth I've understood the power and the effect of time and I respect it more than anything else in the universe.'

'All the more reason not to waste it then.' The girl shifted in the puddle of rainwater that had dripped onto the bare, time-blackened floorboards and sniffed repeatedly and loudly as she stared brazenly at him.

'Oh, look, a Whitehurst,' she said, pointing at the clock. 'I love it. John Whitehurst FRS of Derby — 1713 to 1788. His many achievements included inventing the tell-tale clock and he was one of the finest makers of turret clocks and domestic longcases. He also invented the pulsation engine, as well and —'

‘Yes, yes, yes, clever cogs.’ said Neander with a wit he never knew he possessed. ‘I get it. You know your horologists. Well, it’s a start I suppose.’

‘Does that mean a “yes”?’

‘Not at all. I mean you couldn’t come in to work in a place such as this, dressed like that. You’d badly need to smarten yourself up. And you’d have to do something about that continual sniffing.’

‘I can do that. I would have looked much better this time but I just called in as I was passing by, on the off-chance. I could give you my number so that you can call me when you’ve decided.’

Neander looked thoughtfully at her and frowned. ‘I’ll have a think and let you know.’

‘When?’

‘Don’t push me young lady. I mean it’s not like you’re swamped with opportunities is it? Are you so keen that you can’t afford the time to wait another twenty-four hours? As I said, I’ll be in touch.’

***

Walking up the Oxford Road with his chicken biryani, Neander reflected on something Mr Gastrell had once said to him.

‘Our job is to provide the means for others to order and enjoy their lives, Alexander. We are able provide the mechanism but we can’t control the experience. It’s down to the individual whether or not they make the most of what time they’re given. There’s no value in counting time and storing it away like money. You have to spend it, not horde it. Live in the moment, not the past and certainly not the future. The past is but a memory and the future is but a dream and all we have is the moment. Oh, and try and help others along the way. It makes time go quicker if others around you are happy, believe me.’

Dear old Gastrell. Why had Neander forgotten all of this wisdom that he'd been given so young? Could it be that the purpose of life is to learn these lessons yourself? And could it be that living in the past, or for that matter, the future, stopped these lessons being learnt? Oh well, what was fifty-years in the scheme of things. Time itself had an inexhaustible bank balance full of the stuff. Never too late and all that. Neander looked up at the first star in the clear evening sky and pondered this radiant clockwork universe, its workings a mystery to even an expert like himself.

When he got home, Neander glimpsed himself in the hall mirror and noticed his bad shave from the morning had grown out like a patchy lawn. There was no stopping time. Acting on an impulse, the origin of which unsettled and totally mystified him, he took Mr Faith's business card out of the top pocket of his suit and dropped it dismissively into the waste bin. He then took Hope's blue box with its silver necklace and put it into the back of a safe that was hidden behind a cheaply-framed copper engraving on his dining room wall. "A view of St Olave's, Sickletree, 1771 by Thos. Birchwood". Unbelievably some of the yew trees were still there — their rooty fingers still prying into the innermost secrets of the churchyard's scattered dead. After slamming the door of the safe firmly shut he put the key into a secret drawer in the sideboard. Finally, he opened an empty cigarette packet on the inside of which Amelia Gift had written her number in a cramped hand and put it by the candlestick telephone in the hall. As he hung his damp umbrella on the ugly hat stand that shouldered the dead aspidistra, he made a mental note to tell her there was to be no smoking in the shop during work hours and there was only a half-hour for lunch.

***

Danny Hucklesby rounded the corner where Rosary Lane branched into Basket Hall Road. The traffic was much busier here nowadays. He didn't like loitering on this spot as the noise unsettled him and always made him unconsciously hunch his shoulders and drop his head. The sign that swung out over the junction creaked noisily in the wind and as he lifted his gaze, something important occurred to him and he tapped on the window. He looked beyond the display of cogs, dials, faces and hands and through the workings of the antique turret clock to the daughter of his wife's dead sister. His niece looked up with a start from the mechanical confusion of her workbench and after an instant of recognition gave him a cheery wave. "You alright?" he mouthed and gave her the thumbs up. She answered the question with a smile, a firm nod and a thumbs up of her own. He recalled the conversation that looked like it may have been the turning point in her life.

'What's the point. Now she's gone there's nothing left.'

'There's always a point, Amelia. Never despair. Redemption comes from the most unlikely places and the most unlikely people. Take it from me. I know.'

'I've decided to quit uni.'

'Is that wise?'

'Probably not but I've lost interest.'

'What are you going to do then?'

'Bum around and take drugs.'

'Very funny, but no chance. We owe it to your mum that we don't allow that to happen.'

'I like clocks,' she said after a long time spent studying her feet.

'I know. There's a clockmaker down on the corner —'

'I know. I also know he's a miserable old bastard, so there'll be no opportunity for me there.'

'But he knows his clocks. Allegedly.'

'No chance. It's not even worth talking about.'

'But if he can get you started. Teach you some of his craft —'

'I can't be arsed. I don't need any more rejection, thanks.'

'All I can say again is that you never know where help will come from. My experience is that it's often the strangest of places.'

There was a long reflective pause between the two.

'Okay, I'll drop him a line sometime.'

'Sometime's no good. It's much better to meet face-to-face. His shop'll still be open. Get yourself down there now. No time to lose.'

'It's pissing down with rain, Uncle Danny.'

'No matter. It'll make you look even more keen. And if it helps I can always meet up with him and give you a glowing reference.'

Neander spotted Danny through the glass and his face immediately broke into the broadest of smiles. It was like the grin on the skull of a Jolly Roger — totally incongruous and that was what made it so wonderful. He pointed at Amelia and then at Danny and mimed a clap. Thank goodness he was happy with her.

As he turned to go, for the briefest of moments, Danny's reflection in the glass overlayed the cameo of the smiling duo in the workshop and freeze-framed them together in time. Neander said something to Amelia and a plume of blurred smoke escaped her laughing mouth. (God, he was even letting her smoke).

How will it end for you? Will you stay happy? What will your story be? Meanwhile, the heavy traffic thundered past and drenched the shop's windows with muddy rainwater —

VII / VESPERS

EVENING PRAYER.

‘AT THE LIGHTING

OF THE LAMPS’.

APPROXIMATELY 6PM.

DECLINE

The Barfly

ESME CHECKED HER LEATHERED reflection in the mirror and wondered how she'd ever got this old. This was never meant to have happened. At thirty she always thought she'd never make forty. At forty she thought she'd never make fifty and so on. So where did ninety fit in? Ninety? If she'd known she was going to live this long she would have taken better care of herself. That one always made her laugh. It appealed to her black sense of humour. What was that song? "Enjoy Yourself, (It's Later Than You Think)". Yes, that's it. She hummed a few bars as the lyrics were beyond her. You've still got it up top though, gal. Still as sharp as a tack. In fact, you're so sharp you'll cut yourself. And you can still knock up a mean cottage pie and wash it down with a few home-brews as well. There's plenty of life in the old dog yet. She often spoke to herself like this to ward off an ever-increasing despair. It's a terribly tricky thing is time. First it strips you of everything you have and then it coldly grinds you into dust.

"Time's a great healer". Now that's a laugh. If that was the case why did she feel so knackered all the time? No, that's just old wive's rubbish. Time's a bitch. She ran a finger along a deep furrow on her forehead and sat back down on the couch with her cuppa.

She'd fought the ageing process for so long and tried to make getting to ninety more of a soft landing in a field of long grass rather than a dive headfirst onto tarmac from a great height but by now she'd squeezed every last drop out of life and all she was left with was the dregs. Ninety just didn't bear thinking about. But then, she could look proudly back on her career as the archetypal good-time girl, slinging back the booze like there was no tomorrow and chewing the fat with bits of kids a quarter her age. Gawd, she'd had some great times and that gave her peace as well as her wonderful memories. Nobody could ever accuse her of wasting the time she'd been given or charge her with not living life to the full.

She glanced at the threadbare collection of birthday cards on her mantle piece before picking up the photo album and thumbing through the brittle plastic sleeves that had, like her, clouded with age. Not many of them in here that are around nowadays — just a handful and that would explain why there were fewer cards every year. What was it they said? As you get older the world speeds up and spins so fast around you that it makes you invisible. You can see the world all right, it's just that *it* can't see *you*. Or, if it *can* see you it can't be bothered to let you know. It was her old mate Bunny that had said that before she died. What a drinking buddy she'd been and look, there she was in the album. They'd had some great times together in the bar of the Starlight. That was the place to be back then and what a pub. Crowded every night of the week it was, with free cheese rolls and pickles on Saturday nights and music and meat raffles thrown in during the week. They'd drunk there throughout the Forties to avoid the war, during the Fifties to forget it and finally the Sixties to remember it again. That war just wouldn't go away. It was in the songs they'd sung, the friendships they'd shared and the loves they'd loved. There was no escape from it. It had fashioned them into the people they were and bled the colour from the overcast world they had lived in.

Oh, my Gawd — she'd forgotten she had that photo. There was Lily on the piano and dear old Arthur behind the bar. "Hoo, hoo, hoo, c'mere Esme, you bonnie lass". Now that was someone who knew how to keep a pub — he ran it as a community project to lift the collective spirit and virtually gave the beer away. What was it? About two bob for a Boilermaker? And that was a bottle of brown *and* a pint of mild for the price of a pint. A G and T was the same. No wonder everyone got so plastered every night. We were all drinking half as much more than we could afford thanks to Arthur's kindness. "Aye, the more ye drink, the more ye save", he used to say. A generous Jock. Now, how lucky was that? That had been her life back then. She'd dedicated herself to a cause and that was to have as much fun as possible in the time she'd been given.

She turned another page which revealed another one of her and Bunny. Bless, we looked so young and pretty. And so demure. Just halves of bitter and not the pints you see the young girls slinging back nowadays before they fall arse over tit in the street with their skirt up around their necks. You'd never have behaved like that back then. We were proper ladies. When you drank you kept yourself under control and if you fancied a bit of nooky you went into a field and not up against a lamppost or a wall. Oh yes, she'd seen them all right. They're up to all sorts of nonsense out there nowadays. But back then her and Bunny had been proper ladies. No wonder those old fellas used to slobber all over them. They had looked classy as well as being able to match them drink for drink and joke for joke, dirty or otherwise. Nothing they said

would faze her and Bunny and when they went too far, they would slap those poor old sods as hard as possible for trying to get fresh. You can look but you can't touch Pops. Now it would be great to be just *looked* at by a Grandad let alone touched up by one.

Of course, she'd never regarded drink as a necessity but more as a treat or a pleasure. It was her reward. She didn't want anything else from the world, just half a bitter and a laugh. Not much to ask was it? So what was his problem? What had *always* been his problem? Why had he resented her this one little pleasure? She looked at her cards again and where she'd left a space for the one that was missing. Ninety and you don't send your mother a birthday card. Still what did you expect from the little shit? No wonder I haven't spoken to him and his kids for twenty-five years or more. No wonder she wrote to him that, "You're all dead to me and I never want to see or hear from any of you again". He always knew if he crossed her that would happen so he should have learnt to keep his mouth shut. She was a strong woman and nobody stands between her and having a good time even if he did try to tell her it's for her own good. She was happy enough on her own anyway and there's always her friends. Well, the few who are left.

She wondered how long it had been since she'd had a drink in the Starlight. Too many years, anyway. But tonight they'll have a big shock when she walks in. They'll think she's risen from the grave. She'll show them life *begins* at ninety — there's many a good tune played on an old fiddle and all that. She wondered if they'd still got that Ella Fitzgerald album she used to love.

What was her favourite? Oh, yes, that was it. She sang the first verse of "Every Time We Say Goodbye" softly to herself as she slowly and painfully rose from the chair. She loved that song.

***

She didn't realise how nervous she'd feel doing this. There was a time when this was her daily stroll and it took no more than a few minutes. Actually, twice daily come to think of it. The mornings had been spent on the cooking and cleaning. Gawd, she'd worked hard to get it all done every day and then the partying would be begin as soon as the sun went over the yard arm. She and Melvyn would walk this walk together, hand in hand — just a few hundred yards to the Starlight for a lunchtime session, back for a kip and then back off round there again in the evening until they were either kicked out or allowed a lock-in until the small hours. Then back home for a nightcap or three. She laughed to herself. How did she do it? That was their life together, from day one until the end. She stopped herself thinking about his last painful years. Best keep that one locked away. A gentle snow started to fall and the daylight had nearly gone. She thought about turning back but then remembered she never gave up easily when she had her mind set on something. Especially a good time. She was a strong woman.

She'd hesitated after forcing open the door which seemed to be made of lead — they must have tightened up the springs since she was last here. What a sight she must have made standing in that doorway, swaying and blinking at the bright lights and wincing at the racket. Hardly the entrance she used to make. Back then she'd strut into the place like a young Shirley Bassey making an entrance at the London Palladium.

'What can we do for you darlin'?' said the punk with a pink Mohican at the pool table. 'Rainbow Fields is around the corner.' His mate walked across and held open the door.

Back in the day the punk would have got a mouthful for that greeting but her brash confidence in dealing with liberty-takers had long gone.

'You've forgotten your Zimmer frame, sweetheart.'

Gawd, this place has changed, she thought. No piano, no dartboard, plastic seats and bar and the racket from that bandit in the corner. She walked up to the counter and held on to it for dear life. The room was swaying and so far nobody apart from the pink punk and his mate had even acknowledged her existence. For some reason she'd half expected to have been mobbed by ghosts.

'What'll it be, love?' said the barman.

'Port and lemon, please.'

'Ice?'

'No thanks.'

'Slice of lemon?'

'Yes, please.'

'That'll be twenty-four pence.' He placed the drink on the bar and held out his hand for the money.

Her hand shook as she slowly counted the coins one by one from her purse while the barman drummed his fingers on the bar top as he waited. He looked everywhere apart from at her.

'The last time I was in here that drink would have cost me about one and six,' she said pleasantly. 'It was called the Starlight Inn back then.'

'Really? Well it's the Zoo Bar now, love. Changing times and all that.'

'Arthur worked where you're standing now and a Boilermaker would have cost —'

'Yes, sir?' said the barman to a drunk who'd slammed down his empty glass right next to her.

Esme hobbled over to a spare table and sat on her own amongst the mayhem. Time was when I was the queen of this place. Now there's a ghost in every corner and nothing's left of them all except dust and shadows.

She sipped her drink slowly and took it all in. So, this was what she'd lived for back then. It all seemed a little tacky now. And very noisy, even without her hearing aids. Surely they hadn't made this much noise. The place looked as if it could do with a bloody good do-down-through as well. Her feet had stuck to the carpet as she'd walked in. Disgusting.

'It's Mrs Hucklesby, isn't it?'

'Yes, love. And who are you may I ask?'

'I'm Margo. You're Danny's mum aren't you?'

'Yes, I suppose I am. Or was.'

'Why? has something happened to him?'

'I wouldn't know.'

'I used to go to junior school with him. How's he doing?'

'I don't see or hear that much from him nowadays.' No sense in telling the complete truth. But on the other hand — 'Actually, we haven't spoken in years.'

'Oh, I'm so sorry to hear that.'

'Don't be sorry. It was his decision to leave here and move up country. Got a job, a wife and a couple of kids and suddenly I'm surplus to requirements. What's happened since, I wouldn't know. I don't even know if he's still alive. He'd be nearly seventy by now. All I can say is that it's my birthday today and I haven't had a card or a call from him.'

'Oh dear, that's awful. I don't understand how anybody can do that to their own mum.'

'I used to be the queen of this place you know. Gawd, we had some great times in here.'

'Hang on. I'll get my drink and you can tell me about it.'

The woman picked her drink off another table and whispered something into the ear of a angry looking man who just gave an irritated shrug and carried on talking to his friend.

'Right, you were saying you used to be the undisputed queen of the Zoo Bar.'

'The Starlight Inn.'

'Oh, yeh. I can remember when it was called that.'

'As I said, its my birthday today. My *ninetieth* birthday,' she added proudly.

'Ninety? You're having me on. You don't look it. I hope I'm still coming in here and looking as good as you when I'm ninety.'

No you don't, thought Esme. Being ninety might seem like a nice idea, darling, but nothing more than that. What was it Bunny had said about the world spinning faster and making you invisible?

'Cheers.'

They clinked glasses and took a sip of their drinks.

'Believe me, you don't want to be ninety — sorry what was your name again?'

'Margo.'

'You don't want to be ninety, Margo. When you're young you might but not if and when you get there.' Why spend your days being reminded of a wasted life? A *long* wasted life, she thought.

Good heavens! She saw a young Bunny wave at her from her seat at the bar and then turn back and carry on with her drinking. She stubbed out her cigarette and blew a stream of smoke into the face of an old man that Esme half-recognised and they both creased up with laughter. Bunny waved for Esme to come over and join them. Esme shook her head and mouthed, "In a minute". Bunny just shrugged her shoulders and gave her the thumbs up.

'What's it like? Being ninety. I can't imagine it.'

'Well, I'd put it this way. It's not for the faint hearted, love.'

'I always thought it'd be great to have all my work done and the time to take stock and enjoy myself. Surely that's something isn't it?'

Esme didn't answer. She just looked lost and sat blinking at the flashing lights of the slot machine. And *what* was that music? And why was everyone shouting?

Old Arthur the Jock waved at her from behind the bar and tipped an imaginary glass to his lips. She gave him the thumbs up. He blew her a kiss and she blew one back and he carried on talking with Bunny.

'Please don't be angry and it's none of my business but wouldn't it help if you got in touch with Danny?' said Margo.

'Oh, its way too late for redemption when you're my age,' she said. 'The time for that has long gone and you don't want all the upset. You're just a shell anyway, so why worry. And he's probably forgotten who I am by now — I didn't exactly bother —' She stopped, shocked at her realisation. 'I didn't exactly bother that much myself,' she finished lamely.

Ray and Ruby walked into the bar and brushed the snow off their coats. Dear old Ray and lovely Rubes. She hadn't seen them since Christmas Eve, Gawd-knows-when and here they were and they hadn't aged one bit. Esme raised her glass to them. They both pointed at her with, "Look who it ain't" expressions but didn't come over to speak.

'Excuse me love, only there's a couple of my old mates just come in. I haven't seen them in years.' Margo followed Esme's gaze and looked at the empty space by the door.

'And Gil and Nancy as well. There must be a party tonight. Wonder why I wasn't invited?'

Esme and Margo sat together for a while as the Zoo Bar slowly emptied and people moved on.

'It's time to go,' said Margo. 'Can we walk you home or can I buy you a drink?'

Esme didn't answer at first. She was staring at the floor.

'Hmm? No, it's okay thanks, Bunny. It's only a short walk home. How old do you think I am? Ninety? You cheeky moo!'

'It's Margo,' she said softly and touched her arm. 'Are you sure you're okay?'

'Oh, I'm *fine*. Just *fine*, darling. I'll finish this and be gone. Melvyn'll come and pick me up shortly, I bet. He'll have started thinking I've run off with a Chippendale.'

Margo laughed. 'You're a legend, Mrs Hucklesby.'

(THE BELL RINGS FOR VESPERS)

Esme climbed the six steep steps back up to her house and paused for breath as she fumbled for the key. Something jammed under the door as she opened it and she stooped painfully and picked up a badly creased envelope. She must have missed it from the morning delivery or it had been dropped through the letterbox when she was out.

Dear Mum
Many Happy Returns on your Ninetieth
If you want to call, you can be sure of a warm welcome
With love from Danny, Ellie and the Boys
xxx

She poured herself a nightcap and sat in her chair turning the card over in her hands.

'I told him before. Twenty-five years ago. You *and* your family are all dead to me and dead people don't send birthday cards. Do they, Bunny?'

'Don't do what, my darling?'

'Send people cards. You don't get cards from dead people do you. Have *you* ever had one, Bunny?'

'Certainly not. Dead people don't send cards, letters or even phone for that matter.'

'I thought not. If they did then Melvyn would definitely have been in touch with a postcard.'

'I don't think they've got a postal service down there,' said Bunny and they both hooted with laughter.

'What would he have written?'

'Most probably, "It's your round and mine's a Boilermaker" or something like that.'

'Or, "I'm gagging for an ice-cold lager, it's bloody hot down here".' They both roared.

'Another drink, Bunny, love?'

'Be rude not to, my darling.'

'I'm glad you could come back for a nightcap, Bunny. It's been quite dreary lately. Sometimes I think I'd be happy to just go to sleep and not wake up.'

'That's not like you, Esme. Not like you at all.'

'Well, you said it yourself, Bun, all those years back. I feel invisible. Like I'm not here. Time's up and best get out while the going's good.'

'But if we're in each others hearts then we'll always be together, won't we, darling.'

'Yes, I suppose we will, my love.'

'My opinion, for what it's worth, is that we alienate ourselves for fear of being hurt.'

'Oh, there's all sorts of reasons why we do that,' said Esme to the empty chair.

***

In the unemotional light of dawn Esme mused on the night before. It had been great seeing all of her old friends again and wonder of wonders, she still didn't get hangovers. What a bonus that had been throughout her life, that she could have a good session and still wake up as fresh as a daisy. That was what had made her the legendary drinker she was. That girl in the Starlight had said it last night. "You're a legend, Mrs Hucklesby". Well, yes, she bloody well was. She was a *ninety*-year-old legend. She took a reflective sip from her morning cuppa and something caught her eye. Oh, she'd forgotten that. She snatched at the unwanted birthday card and snorted as she tore it in half and threw it in the bin with a dramatic flourish and a distasteful expression. It was as if it had been sent from someone or somewhere unpleasant.

This was what she'd been waiting for all these years. Victory. And it tasted as sweet as the first port and lemon of the night. She'd stood her ground and won. How dare he even think of standing up to her and trying to stop her having a good time, the cheeky little sod. She'd give him, "It'd be for your own good, Mum". Well, she had some news for him. She was back.

"Never trust a man who doesn't drink", Melvyn had told her and boy, was he right. Even if it does happen to be your own son. There was only going to be one outcome when anyone stood in the way of her having a good time. But then, she was a strong woman after all.

VIII / COMPLINE

NIGHT PRAYER.

BEFORE RETIRING.

APPROXIMATELY 7PM.

EXTINCTION

In Limbo

THE OLD MAN SAT in the garden surrounded by the remnants of Her. The oxeye daisies that She had planted in memory of Marnie and the honeysuckle were still fresh and blooming after all this time. The countless terracotta flowerpots had been neglected for many a year, as they always provoked bittersweet memories, but he was not brave or strong enough to give them away. They huddled together in sunny corners filled with nothing except cakes of arid and impotent compost, their life-enhancing energy spent. The desiccated holly leaves on the path had been shaped into a crown of thorns by the summer breezes, deadly if mishandled. A solitary blackbird, probably the son, of a son, of a son of the bird that had whistled a goodbye song on the day She had left was enjoying the crumbs of oat biscuit the old man had scattered on the lawn the day before.

'They're Marnie,' She had said about the white daisies. She had repeated this mantra every year when the flowers were in full bloom. 'That beautiful little girl.' It was as if She believed, after it was said to him often enough, that the penny would finally drop and they could both embrace the healing power of acceptance. He had never really understood exactly what She had meant by linking the girl with the flowers, thinking they were just a token of her short life. But he did now.

'They're that beautiful little girl's consciousness reborn every summer,' he was told. He understood that now and the thought gave him a degree of peace.

He had been waiting and reflecting alone for a very long time. Quite how long he wasn't sure as time was not so easily tracked nowadays. He knew when She had left and he knew today's date and he still had the wits to work it out in his head, but no matter. It was a long time and that fact he knew and that was pain enough. He'd discovered that Limbo is a strange and demanding place and finding the meaning or purpose of a life is a hard thing to do without lying to oneself. At the time it had all been so clear and natural. Work, fun, eat, sleep, love, in no particular order except Work. Always Work first. Now the Work had gone. And the fun and the love. Now he just ate and slept. If he had realised it was going to be like this he might have paid more attention but that was one thing he'd never had the time and talent for as there had always been Work as a means to deflect his focus from the truly important aspects of life. He regarded old age as an insult and not, like others, as a blessing. You can't do what you want to do. You can't Work. He took a sip of tea and tried to stay in the moment, away from the fearful future and the mostly forgotten past that deceived him daily.

He picked up the lonely letter that had arrived on the doormat that morning and read the message on the back.

This envelope contains information about a funeral plan.
If it has arrived at an inappropriate time we sincerely apologise and ask you to dispose of the mailing.

He angrily threw the letter unopened onto the garden table where last night's raindrops quickly bled the address back into the paper. Every time is inappropriate for that shit, he mused.

A cooling breeze stirred the buddleia and its surrounding insect life into drowsy wakefulness. Unknown to him a bee swarm had gathered under the tree and was busy starting a colony. It often occurred to him how many creatures that don't have the concept of ownership shared his home. Millions upon millions of them. And you think you own this space? He chuckled to himself.

He recalled a scene from an old film where the time machine sat motionless in a room and the world accelerated around it. This concept had always fascinated him. The machine and the room stayed the same but time ran through and around it and changed everything. So what had time changed here? The flowers had bloomed and returned to the earth, walls had turned green, crumbled and fallen and people and animals had come and gone in the blink of an eye. But the machine and the space remained the same. He saw himself as the time machine and the garden as the room. So, again, what had time changed? He closed his eyes and played the film over in his head.

The credits rolled with the departure of the old lady who had lived in the house for a similar timespan as the old man. She returned an instant later and stared through the gate at the garden, alone in a transient winter twilight. He freeze-framed her in the gloom, zoomed in and studied her bewildered expression as she looked back on the life that had been hers, once-upon-a-time in yesterday.

A touch of the time machine's controls and the old lady instantly disappeared leaving only her glowing silhouette on the old man's retina. A hysterical mistle thrush skated along a frosted wall and the blood-red holly berries were stripped from bottom to top over and over again. Dead or lost family members were ushered in and out of the gate while forgotten friends came and went and then left the stage forever, callously edited out of the script by that unforgiving editor, time. A petite tabby cat arrived unannounced, gleefully chased mice and starlings and died on the lawn under the pear tree in the instant it took the old man to remember her name.

The film was fast-forwarding now at an unbelievable speed, a week in a heartbeat, a lifetime in a moment. Leaves carpeted the grass, followed by stroboscopic flashes of deep snows and blinding suns, as intermittent moons waxed and waned and laid bare their pale, rhythmic, mysterious order. Families of hedgehogs sprinted across the starlit lawn and an ancient apple tree fell with a crash and was callously dismembered and hauled away in pieces. Every few seconds the pulsing laburnum burst into yellow magnificence against a crystal sky, its slow demise a thing of utmost sadness. Two small boys appeared and grew quickly. Too quickly. One lay in a hammock, dreaming while the other threw a tennis ball over and over against the wall and grew tall in the process. They chased each other around the garden on skateboards and bikes and covered the prefab garage with graffiti. The old man heard guitars and drums — music to his ears now, but not, as he remembered, at the time.

He saw time itself as it sped faster blurring day and night into a half-light and through it all there he was, leaving and returning, leaving and returning, with a mechanistic precision, to and from Work and looking ever more jaded and preoccupied by his world as he did so. The two boys, now grown men, disappeared out of the voracious jaw of the gate that incessantly opened and shut and mindlessly consumed souls as it did so. Their reappearances grew fewer and when they did return it was in sporadic fleeting instances with ever-longer pauses. No younger children appeared to take their place. And all the while She was always there, tending flowers that blossomed and crumbled, bloomed and withered in her loving hands. Then, like a flower, She too blossomed, faded and withered and She and her flowers were gone as well.

The film moved onwards, the plot not yet revealed. Visitors stopped coming through the gate. The neighbourhood became rougher with wrecked cars abandoned on pavements and untended dogs running in the lane. A van he didn't recognise swung into the drive in the twilight and shadowmen with torches emptied the garage. Litter careered down the street in ever increasing amounts and the pavements crumbled and sprouted weeds; a larchlap fence flew away in pieces and only the gap endured; windows were painted in hideously garish colours; doors remained closed and unwanted fridges and washing machines decorated gardens and lawns. Towers of black plastic bags spiralled skywards; people stopped walking and the manic traffic flourished in their place; the grass grew long on lawns that had once been obsessively manicured along with a show of packaging, bin bags and cans in the borders. Front gardens sprouted carelessly parked cars and ugly gravel instead of flowers, hedges and lawns. In apparently no time, an air of dejection and neglect hung over the lane while security lights flashed on and off as their fearfully watchful beams probed obsessively and needlessly into the empty nights.

By now even the paper boy, dustman, milkman and postman had stopped appearing and the only visitor was an unfamiliar stranger who tottered infrequently into the garden and pottered around. Who was it? Either way, he looked like he was struggling badly with his walking and he looked so very pale, worried and unhappy. Who's the hell's that for heaven sake? thought the old man. Fancy letting that poor old sod fart around with that mower. Look at him struggling to clear the front path of snow. He can hardly lift that spade. What a state to get into. Oh, give it up for Christ's sake, you're making me feel ill. The decrepit figure appeared progressively more feeble every time it reappeared. It got to a situation where it was almost laughable it was so pathetic. 'Give in mate,' the old man shouted at him. 'Who are you?' His white hair grew more unkempt and his beard more wild with each appearance. It was just then, when he had overseen more than half-a-century of growth, death and decay and when he had started to become irritated by the man's courage and valiant determination not to admit defeat, that he realised that it was his almost unrecognisable self.

There followed a long, empty twilight. So long in fact, the old man thought that the film had ended, until a solitary hedgehog scuttled across a winter lawn in a half-light and left a faint trail of indigo pawprints in the snow. You should be hibernating, Fuzzpig, thought the old man. Snug as a bug in a rug with your family. Time to get some rest — I know just how you feel. The hedgehog walked up to the old man's time machine, sniffed around and then, like everything else in the film, disappeared forever into nothingness. It was then that the old man saw through the illusion. All of the appearances and departures, the endless comings and goings, the hellos and goodbyes were just different aspects of the same thing. Whatever that thing was he didn't have a clue but these endless manifestations had a common source. Like a tree that blossomed in the spring and died at the end of each year only to be reborn time and again, under all of this change, its essence was the same. So, Marnie *is* those daisies after all. She *had* been right about that all along and he thanked her for showing him that last great truth. He finally understood it now and it brought him closure. Salvation comes in many guises thought the old man: mine has come through a solitary hedgehog on a cold winter night, with its spines set courageously against a threatening world. Which was so perfectly appropriate it made him laugh out loud.

And now the film spooled and he was back in the moment. This moment. The only one they say there ever is. He sat for a while and reflected on all that he had seen. After a moment of brutal self-analysis he came to another understanding; all of the love and time he had been given had been lost. This realisation, unrecoverable and dreadful as it was meant he now knew there had been only one chance to treasure all that life had given him. He couldn't even replay his film to bring it back because, like sand, love and time just trickled through your fingers and disappeared forever. There was, he discovered, no rewind button on the time machine and that, at the end, we are left with nothing but echoes and shadows of the eternal moment.

(THE BELL RINGS FOR COMPLINE)

He was sitting by Marnie as the Visitor walked through the elmwood gate. He was the most ordinary looking man you ever saw — everyone's companion, a face on a crowded street, so easily ignored and passed by. Dressed from head to toe in black he stood in respectful silence on the path and studied the old man calmly as he carefully picked a fallen holly leaf from his shoulder. The old man ignored him, looking anywhere but in his direction.

'Mr Daniel William Hucklesby?' asked the Visitor as he ran a finger over his clipboard.

'What kept you?' said the old man irritably.

'Yes, I know I'm late, but I doubt if you're sorry about that. We like to do the impatient ones first. The ones that've had enough and want to get it over with. You seemed happy enough to wait.'

'Can I finish my tea please?'

'No, we're on a tight schedule.'

'You've only just taken my father.'

'That makes no difference.'

'And my mother.'

'What's your point, sir?'

'Well, I thought it would mean you wouldn't be back for quite a while.'

'As I said, that makes no difference. I thought you'd have realised that by now.'

'Are you sure?'

'Well, you've just seen the film and you know what they say about your life flashing before your eyes —'

The old man rose creakily to his feet. The heat took his legs and he wobbled. That was all it took nowadays. He hobbled slowly towards the Visitor who smiled kindly at his pained progress but didn't move to help him. The strange numbness in his feet that they had never got to the bottom of made every step feel like he was walking barefoot on splintered wood.

'Sorry, but getting around is difficult these days.'

'No matter. Take your time.'

He looked back and saw himself dead asleep by the garden table, head thrown back and mouth wide open. What a state to get into. In the border next to Marnie he noticed for the first time a solitary bright red poppy had grown through the weeds.

'I must pick that,' said the old man. 'It'll seed and before you know it they'll be covering the garden.'

'As I said, there's no more time.'

'Where are we going?' asked the old man.

'Home, sir,' said the Visitor. 'You're going home.'

'But *this* is home.'

'Are you sure?' said the Visitor.

'Of course I'm sure. I've lived here for —'

He tailed away as the years escaped him.

'Not any more,' said the Visitor and he placed his hand gently and firmly in the small of the old man's back and steered him slowly towards the gate.

'You do have a lot left to learn,' added the Visitor. 'Ownership, if you want to call it that, is only temporary.' He made a note on his clipboard which read, "Still doesn't understand possession".

'Do I have to go?' asked the old man. 'I'm very tired and don't like to travel far any more.'

'That's exactly why I'm here.'

There was a black Mercedes immaculately parked on the drive with its back passenger door open. This was exciting. He hated driving so much nowadays that he had become marooned on an island in a sea of green, his driving licence an unused passport to exotic places.

'Thanks for driving me — I hope I'm no trouble.'

'You're not any trouble at all. It's my job. Just walk through the gate. There's some people waiting for you that I think you'll be happy to see.'

'Oh, okay then. I could do with some company.'

'Yes, it'll do you good.'

'Could do with a natter with old Steve.'

'The Visitor thought for a moment. 'Can I say something?'

'And there was me thinking you were in a hurry. Okay, go on. I've plenty of time.' The old man rolled his eyes.

'If there's one thing I've learnt in my job is that you spend your whole life training for a fight which you're always going to lose. How's that for being unfair? No wonder so many think, why bother, and throw in the towel. But you never did that.'

As he turned back for one last look at the house the old man noticed an excitable young family walk straight past him and through the open gate without saying a word. Pretty rude, he thought — they just ignored me completely. Not even a "hello". Just like I wasn't there. Bloody cheek. The family stood together in the garden, nodding and laughing at each other as they stared in appreciation at his home. The man swept the boy into his arms and the woman put her hand on the girl's shoulder and pointed at the front door and said something to her. The little girl jumped up and down on the spot with excitement, her knees almost up to her chest, her long hair covered her face in sweeps of the palest of golds. The baton had been passed on. Such joy. Yes, *joy.* He had almost forgotten the meaning of the word let alone the feeling. It was then he discovered how cathartic letting go can be.

The old man watched the father take a key from his pocket and open the front door. He then picked up his wife and carried her over the threshold and into the darkness of the porch. The little boy took a photo with his mobile phone and showed it to the girl who jumped for joy once again.

'Sorry but you'll have to leave that.' The Visitor indicated a brassy looking ring on the old man's slender corrugated finger.

'But She gave me that. Years ago, on our wedding day.'

'You can't bring any possessions with you, only the clothes you're standing in. That was made clear from the start. Oh, and a bunch of flowers.'

'Flowers? I don't like flowers.'

'Yes, flowers. You've seen them haven't you?'

'Well, what shall I do with it?'

'That's up to you, sir. Some people like to hide their things for others to find.' He indicated the little girl with the butternut hair.

The ring slipped off his emaciated finger so easily it almost fell into his palm.

'Should have made plans, sir.'

'I didn't expect —'

'They seldom do.'

The old man nodded acceptance, bent painfully and hid the ring and some loose change under a drift of dead leaves. He then walked slowly back to the border and picked the poppy.

'I've got my flower.'

The visitor nodded. 'Ready for some new adventures, sir?'

'Yes, ready. He took a deep breath. 'I read somewhere that death is nothing more than the popping of a bubble and that we are separated from eternity by something as thin and fragile as the skin of a balloon.' The old man smiled to himself as he got into the car and fitted the seatbelt.

'I wouldn't know about that, sir,' said the Visitor as he put the car into gear and pulled smoothly out of the drive. 'I'm just the driver. Somebody in the philosophy department might be able to help on that one. All I can tell you is that nearly all of my clients have more questions than answers by the time I visit them.'

The old man didn't look back as they drove away.

'We just disappear in a cloud of stardust and all that remains are echoes and shadows of the eternal moment —'

'Well put, sir,' said the Visitor. 'Just echoes and shadows of the eternal moment. I like that.'

In fine diei

*This book is a gift and one of a limited edition.
If you have enjoyed its pages it would be appreciated
by the author, illustrator and editor if you could make an
appropriate donation to a mental health charity of your choice.*

BONUS STORY

Keep Buggering On!

WITH MILITARY PRECISION EVERY Tuesday evening at six on the dot the card school of the Sickletree Conservative Association gathered in the taproom of the Wonky Donkey in the town's Market Square to gossip, cheat, moan, rant and sometimes even play the occasional hand of whatever game took the players fancy on the night. To say the cards were inconsequential would be stretching it a little as an element of competition between the players did exist but it was one of their unwritten rules that the cards were of secondary importance to the jaw-jaw and the conversations, once begun, were encouraged to meander in any direction and on any subject of interest. Politics, whether local, national or international, were special favourites of course, especially the disturbing cult of cultural and historical revisionism that was currently trickling out of the universities and a clique of other less elevated educational institutions and puzzling the nation with its bizarre logic as it did so. Everything that this proud country had achieved and stood for was being put under the microscope, reevaluated and repositioned by kids who hadn't even been alive when most of what they were trying to change had originated and nothing was regarded as sacrosanct. National heroes, traditions, the social order, the English language, law enforcement, national identity, you name it and it was, or soon would be, under attack from these purveyors of progressive propaganda and misinterpretation.

(THE BELL RINGS FOR VESPERS)

As landlord of the pub and the originator of the group, Major Tappy Fawceytt, chaired proceedings with a geniality and humility which were the hallmarks of his character and directed the discourses with all of the subtle influence and powers of persuasion of a master of misinformation.

There he sat, at the head of a beer-soaked table, a far cry from the brash young paratrooper who had been decorated for gallantry at Arnhem so many years before. Over the time that followed the ending of his exemplary military career, Tappy had slowly squandered a massive inheritance and, following a deep despair about what he saw as the backward trajectory of the country he loved, had permitted himself to go to seed at the same time. This had ultimately brought on a depression so deep and overwhelming that, upon rising one morning, Tappy had decided that he had lost the will to walk and without a second thought confined himself to life in a wheelchair. And that was just the beginning of his downward spiral. He grew fat, abandoned basic personal hygiene and lost what little interest in his appearance he'd ever had. He allowed his iron-grey hair to sprout sparse and lank from a head the shape and colour of a bruised russet apple and his nicotine-tinted facial fungus was given *carte blanche* to spread insidiously over his sagging chest. His armpits flaked, his feet stank; he was, in short, a mess. But a spark of his old dignity and spirit was often reignited at these Tuesday meetings and his passionate discordance with the direction and behaviour of the modern world meant that, for an hour or two, he often became the Tappy of old — that is, a man with fire, purpose and a mission in life.

***

'Ladies and Gentlemen, her Madge the Queen.' Tappy pushed back his aviator glasses onto the bridge of his nose with a plump forefinger, doffed his battered fez and raised a quarter-full pint mug of slop and froth to the yellowed ceiling.

There was a prolonged scraping of chairs on the flagstone floor. 'The Queen,' replied the assembly vigorously.

'And while you're standing, it was on this very day, five years ago, that my dear old quaffing compadre, Buggles, left his bar stool never to return. So, dear friends, please also raise your jar to the Quaffer in Chief, in whatever corporeal form and whichever corner of this beautiful universe he may currently be imbibing.'

This directive wasn't met with any obvious enthusiasm from the gathering. Exactly the opposite, in fact.

'He's out of his skull on the planet Blotto, no doubt,' said a stout woman in a stiff blue jacket. 'Dreadful little man. Should have been gelded at birth.' She sniffed dismissively, flicked nervously at her severe white bob and sat back down without raising her glass. She glared at Tappy through her winged, cat-eye specs.

'Come now Catty, old girl. Don't be mean. Generosity of spirit and all that. He *was* my bestest pal after all said and done.'

'Unpleasant toad of a man. Who could ever forget when he soiled himself in front of the Mayor at the Rotary's Fruits of the Ocean scampi and chips evening.' Kitty Cathcart, Head of Women's Engagement at the SCA was not to be persuaded.

'Ah. Forgive and forget though, Catty. Dear old Buggles.'

'He used to call me "his Pussy". How can one ever forgive him for that? *His* Pussy. As if,' snorted Catty.

'Or forget his constant cheating at dominoes,' added a bull-like man in a dung-splattered Barbour as he twiddled the wiry black whiskers that grew from his glowing cheekbones. His face looked as if it had been laminated with pigskin.

'Surely not you as well, Archie. I'd always assumed that the milk of human kindness would have been a touch more prevalent in a dairy farmer,' said Tappy.

'Repulsive man. He came on strong to me in the snug one night. Tried to put his furry tongue in my mouth.' Catty had unfinished business with the desecration of the reputation of Tappy's dear, departed friend.

'Was he still attached to it at the time?' asked Archie.

'TMI, Catty dear,' said Tappy. 'Never speak ill and all that.'

'All round bad egg. Always welched on rounds, bills and gambling debts,' offered Archie by way of summary.

'Archie Grubber, you know full well that dear old Buggles was always short of funds and that he was adept at his own brand of creative accountancy.' Tappy sadly shook his apple-head and took a sip of beer which sloshed a half-moon of grey foam onto his tash.

'What about when he took on the whole of that female stag party from Brummagem in a yard of ale contest? "Bring me your finest drinker you Brummie slags", he hollered at the top of his voice before he collapsed in the urinals.' Archie's heavy shoulders rose and fell as he silently chuckled at the memory.

'He spent the rest of the night singing rugger songs whilst concurrently creating a horribly foetid lavatorial funk in the bar. Good value was old Buggles,' said his only fan.

'He always smelt like that. Never changed his underpants — allegedly,' offered Catty with another disdainful sniff.

'*Au contraire*. They were changed once a month whether he needed to or not,' confided Tappy gently.

'Didn't he fiddle the thrift? Allegedly.'

'No, that was a total misunderstanding,' said Tappy, desperately waggling a forefinger. 'The money was found in the end.'

'Yeh, in his back pocket.'

'Peddled his bike home — full of ale — in the wrong direction — up a one-way-street. Hence he is now *kaput* and being spoken of in the past tense. No sympathy for the man, I'm afraid.' Catty crossed her arms and shrugged.

'Come to think of it, Tappy. Didn't you and he have handbags-at-dawn over his unpaid bar tab?' offered a fourth member of the party from behind an enormous, outdated handlebar moustache.

'Never, Hugo. Buggles was as straight as a die.'

'I'm sure I heard that you and he had words.'

'Dearest Buggles, QiP. Quaff in Peace old friend.'

Tappy clumsily unpacked a new deck of cards from its cellophane wrapping with his pudgy fingers. He shuffled them with a degree of dexterity that indicated long practice in the art and dealt seven cards to each member of the school. He then flipped the top card on the remaining stack to reveal a naked monochrome lady with the three of hearts trapped in her eye-watering cleavage.

'Are you sure these cards are actually legal, Light of My Life?' shouted Tappy to a horse-faced woman with vacant eyes who was huffing and buffing wine glasses behind the counter of the empty bar room. 'I know she's old enough to be Methusela's grandmama but that makes it even more distasteful in a way.'

'I wouldn't know, Dear Heart. I got fifty packs of them from a car boot sale at the Guide's jamboree. They'll last you all year.'

'Excellent woman,' said Tappy. 'In that case I should imagine we're in the clear from the Sickletree Vice Squad. Knockout whist it is then players? Tits — I mean hearts — are trumps.'

'Oh Tappy, really. Have you seen the eight of clubs? You could never play beach volleyball with a pair like that.'

'Don't give your hand away, Arabella old girl. I shall peruse the naked babushkas later at my leisure. Stay focused for now, eh?'

A half-hour later the door was flung open and the first customer of the evening walked into the bar.

'Hroooow!' yowled Tappy to the newcomer.

'Hroooow!' yowled the newcomer back.

'Is that your mating call?' asked Catty.

'It's Felix the Cat. Where've you *been*?' asked Tappy. 'Come and join in, quick, but have a *shufti* at these first.' Tappy flashed a card and Felix nodded in appreciation.

'As you're no doubt well aware, you don't get many of those to the pound, old chum, so you'd better get stuck in right away. Tits are trumps.'

'Ding, *dong*. I think in her case it's *derrières* that are trumps,' said Felix. 'You're looking well, Tappy. Been anywhere nasty?'

'We're just back from Morocco, thoroughly revitalised and refreshed. Which is why I am sporting a fez and djellaba.' Tappy indicated his stained, tattered and beautifully decorated robe.

'Well, *salaam effendi* to you, old boy!' Felix touched his forehead and bowed low. He struggled to return to the vertical.

'No, seriously. The memsahib and I have bought a shedload of Arabic threads on the cheap and will be selling them at car boot sales at a location near you this summer.'

'Djellaba great time?' asked Felix. 'D'ya get it?'

'Not really,' said Tappy. 'But I digress. We have also smuggled in a wonderful selection of Moroccan spices, bought in bulk from the casbah, for your delectation.'

'Oh, Tappy, sweet. Save me some turmeric please. My spicy tandoori chicken is to die for and it's so good for my arthritis,' said Arabella and with her seductive olive eyes she flashed a set of eyelashes that looked as if they'd been treated with coal tar.

'You have but to demand and the mysteries and fruits of the Orient will be laid at your dainty tootsies, Oh My Beloved Sultana.'

'Peace be upon you, Oh My Beneficent Overlord, Master of the Bedchamber and High Barsteward. Shall we meet at the back of the harem to do the business?'

'And peace be upon you as well, Oh Star of the Morning. That'll be thirty-seven Moroccan dirhams for the turmeric, by the way, or two quid in old money.'

'So sorry to interrupt this scene from *A Thousand and One Arabian Nights* but you still owe us for the bag of cumin we brought back for you last time, Arabella,' shouted Pippa Fawceytt from behind the bar. No more stash without the cash, *Habiibi*. Sorry!'

'Oh, let's get on with it for crissake,' shouted Hugo. 'Archie to deal and tits, I mean *clubs*, are trumps.'

'Time for a break,' said Tappy. 'Whose round is it?'

The group sat in gratified silence and stuffed the ham and cheese toasties and slices of pork pie and gherkins that Pippa had materialised from behind the bar.

'What are those pics on the wall? — those over there, Tappy — I've never noticed them before,' asked Hugo between munches.

Tappy rolled his wheelchair over to a wainscoted wall, pointed at the display with a rattan cane and loudly cleared his throat.

'This newspaper cutting is the front page of the Grauniad's General Election Special when I stood as an Independent in the Sickletree by-election. I didn't win of course but didn't finish last and best of all, we had the finest bar at the results thingy! In fact we had the *only* bar at the results thingy. Of course Nigel Hoggard, that oily official Tory, was easily returned by his hordes of fawning lackeys and then promptly crossed the floor to Labour. How one does abhor a quisling.'

'Oh, bloody hell, not this again,' said Archie. 'Can we get back to the cards? Please?'

'If I remember, each candidate was allowed two representatives to attend the count and make sure there was no cheating. I was one of yours, Tappy and what a dry old business that turned out to be — watching grey people counting ticks and crosses. However, in true Tappy style we improved it by setting up a bar in the corridor and all were invited. Every candidate attended except that defector — or should that be defecator? — Hoggard. As I recall, you got quite a few votes, Tappy.' said Felix.

'Spot on, Felix. They did all come and have a snorter. Labour — can't recollect the name, the delightful Darren Alsop of the Flying Carpet Brigade — Natural Law, Dermot Rugg — Liberals. The Greens had some woman whose name escapes me. That turncoat bastard, Hoggard, rudely declined. I recall being interviewed by the Home Service afterwards and thought they were recording it. When asked what were the main differences between Hoggard and myself, I replied, "Six pints of ale, at least half a bottle of cognac and about four stone". Oh dear — it was live! Funny old night.'

'I did ham and lettuce sandwiches,' said Pippa half to herself. She had joined them for the refreshments and was absently nibbling a cheese straw between sips of her vodka and tonic.

'So you did,' said Tappy as he patted her leg condescendingly. 'And very fine they were too, with lashings of Colemans and plenty of butter and pepper. Now would you be so kind as to wheel me off to the karzi to water the greens and I will probably need help with giving the old One-Eyed Trouser Snake a good shake as well.'

'The other is a pic of the Artillery Ball, 1947 with Pater and Mama idling away the post-war days at The Ritz,' resumed Tappy after he'd been wheeled back into the circle sporting a prominent damp patch on the crotch of his trousers. 'Pater, front, Mama opposite.'

'We're here for the bloody cards not *All Our Yesterdays*.'

'Thank you, Archie. I will keep you but a moment longer.'

'Great pic. Was going to ask which ones are your parents, but one look at the face of the chap with the tash was enough to tell me,' said Felix.

'Great Scot! I got your mama right, but that was just amateur guesswork,' said Hugo. 'I took your papa to be Tyrone Power and instead I gave the chap next to him a balding head and an out-of-control beard and came up with you!'

'No, that's Uncle Squeaky. Dead ringer for Pater apart from the cleft-lip,' said Pippa.

'Are you sure?' asked Felix. He does look an awful lot like Tappy, cleft-lip or no.'

'It's just a family resemblance, old boy. What *are* you inferring?' snapped Tappy tetchily. 'You don't half keep on sometimes, don't you? Just let it go for once.'

This outburst was followed by a protracted silence as the card school either studied the floor or chewed innocently on the last of the sausage and bacon rolls.

'Right,' said Hugo after a long pause. 'Let's get back to the business of the evening.' He lit a lung-blitzing Craven A, slipped it into the corner of his mouth and dealt briskly at the same time as suppressing an evil sounding cough. 'And tits are trumps again. Hoorah!' he croaked. 'Tits are always trumps.'

The game proceeded in an embarrassed silence for several minutes until it was interrupted by Tappy violently throwing his hand into the middle of the table.

'Oh, I don't know what's the matter with me. The rain has been falling in stair rods and I've been bitten by the Black Dog and I don't mean Pongo Fawceytt the Third of that lineage — although him passing water on the antimacassar this morning didn't help.

Last night, in order to lift my spirits I watched *Reach for the Sky* once again, and it worked on a temporary basis. As Bader said, "Where can I buy a Spitfire?" and, like him, I badly need something to cheer me up. Sadly, on reflection, all watching old Douglas did in the end was to make me even more despondent about what a mess this country's in. There's no magic left, just despondency.'

'I wouldn't listen to Douglas,' said Archie. 'He's always getting legless anyway.'

Tappy gave him a pointed look but said nothing, preferring to continue with his jaundiced view of the state of the nation.

'There is nobody left with the *cojones* to make a decision any more. Everything is done by sodding committee which has left the country utterly jaspered. I have now reluctantly arrived at the conclusion that I don't actually give a tinkers cuss any longer. I've always tried to help people, employed thousands of staff, collected millions in tax, tried to be kind and compassionate to everyone I meet but I can't cope with the enfeeblement of this sceptred isle. Sod them all. I'm struggling to Keep Buggering On —'

'Not sure about the tax millions boast,' said Archie.

'I left school at fifteen with passable games of rugger and cricket but, more importantly, with an invaluable knowledge of our mother tongue. I learnt how to add up and how to behave politely in society. Every other attribute I possess has been acquired in the University of Life. I have encountered fiscal peaks and troughs without the benefit of the input of any family mazuma.' He had conveniently overlooked his inheritance in order to make a point.

'Yes, I am excited by the progress that has been made in the field of medicine and, yes, as a species we have put men on the moon, invented computers — though is that such a good thing one asks oneself? — explored the farthest flung boundaries of our planet and brewed an infinite variety of delectable real ales. I jest.

All that said, there are several issues that upset me, the biggest of which is the NHS where the front line medicos and nursing staff are nothing short of heroic but the administration is wildly top heavy and disjointed. I find this particularly irksome and totally against the ethos and spirit of its formation.'

'Hear, hear,' muttered Archie and he slapped the table with his huge farmer's hand.

'Controversially, I would like to see or hear Alvar Lidell back on the BBC National News. Regional accents are fair game on regional programmes but sadly I miss being able to understand most newscasters. Sorry, but that's how it is.'

'The media try to portray a world that is unrecognisable even to me and I'm younger than you, Tappy. You have to realise that only a marginal amount of people actually believe in this new world vision and the reason you feel the way you do is that a small amount of people are making a lot of noise. Trust me, you are not alone in your confusion and misery. KBO!' said Felix.

The whole card school began pumping their fists in the air and chanting "K-B-O" to the alarm of the drinkers in the bar.

'Yes, sadly, I'm afraid that's the case. I have recently been cancelled by a close family member which is pretty horrific and am constantly being attacked for my somewhat archaic attitudes and my belief in politeness. This happens with monotonous regularity — in commerce, hospitals, shops and often, even in the street. So yes, I come across it in real life all the time. Fortunately my idiot's lantern only plays black and white British films from the 1940s and before which I find a consolation. I avoid stations such as the ITV and never answer the phone — it's face-to-face that counts.'

'Fortunately my idiot's lantern only plays porn,' said Felix with a sly grin. 'Don't assume the world is what you see through your rectangular device. Your world is what's outside your front door!

Has anyone really cancelled you in real life? Is there anyone who is truly offensively racist? Is anyone literally being that politically correct person you speak of? I would say, probably not! So, stop letting the fake world you see through your plastic thing rule the life you live. It's all just smoke and mirrors.'

'Don't worry, Tapps. There's still the occasional Luddite like my good self who just gets on with things, likes to help people and, by Jove, are prepared to ask a woman of child-bearing age when she's at a job interview if she plans on getting pregnant,' said Hugo.

'I've been bingewatching the Olympics and there's been far too much blubbing on the podium for my liking. It's the chaps I'm talking about, not the ladies. One expects the fairer sex to become emotional *in extremis* but not hairy-gorilla weightlifter bods with a set of gonads the size and density of medicine balls,' said Tappy.

The group concurred.

'Girls become boys and boys become girls, it's a messed up, mixed up, topsy-turvy world. Wasn't that a song?'

'Any medals should be confiscated and melted down for scrap.'

'Agreed. These mummy's boys are letting the country down.'

'Today's young have been neutered. Most don't know if they're Arthur or Martha without checking the undercarriage.'

Their attention momentarily drifted back to the game and several hands were played in silence until Tappy indicated he was still not in a frame of mind to let things lie.

'And as an epilogue to my eternal rant — thank you so very much to the microcephalus dunderhead, who would undoubtedly have been a rabid lackey and follower of the Little Corporal with a toothbrush moustache, for his jobsworth imbecility in the home of the Immortal Bard a while back. On being ejaculated from the Horsepiddle for the second time for lack of beds, we stopped on Waterside for a coffee and parked in the disabled bay. Sadly, the badge was the wrong way round as the mindless authorities insist on it being displayed a certain way and I forgot to change it. Outcome — protestations ignored! Cha-ching! I am now twenty-five quid lighter. Shame on you Warwickshire County Council!'

'Appeal m'dear. There is enough suffering already in the world without being ejaculated by a lowly trafficator,' said Catty.

'Sadly, Catty, my righteous and darling guardian angel, I am all out of energy. Bollo to them, each and every one!' said Tappy.

'That is toolery in its most resplendent pugnacious tenacity. I hope the trafficator runs out of lavatory paper during his morning ablutions and has to walk to the nearest convenience in his soiled undergarments whilst enduring a somewhat uncomfortable and embarrassing spell of self inflicted karma in the process.'

'An excellent comment, Hugo, dear boy, and thank you for that creative and imaginative musing. It has given me a degree of comfort and assurance in my fiscal and emotional despair,' said Tappy with deep feeling.

'What happened at the Horsepiddle, Tappy? asked Archie.

'Well, as you can see, I am glad to say that I am now liberated and safely back at home. The staff really were extremely pleasant and kind and were carrying out their duties in difficult times. The ward, through no fault of the staff, did appear to morph into something akin to *One Flew Over the Cuckoo's Nest* at times. I think even a short time spent in such an environment encourages an Alcatraz type of institutionalised behaviour. Anyway, I digress — I had the "Gobocam" and am glad to report that things seem in good order up top. I was then transferred for an "Arsocam" to see what was happening in my capacious lower regions. I actually prefer the "Arsocam" to the "Gobocam" so wasn't worried by this, though of course I had to make sure that I didn't actually enjoy it.'

'I too have had the northbound *and* southbound inspections, and I can assure you it is not something one would deposit in the Wank Bank. My results did however find future problems which were resolved. So whilst it is not a masturbatory experience, the value of the procedure is worth the discomfort, humiliation and derogatory comments from the uninitiated.' Felix casually flicked onto the stack a beaming beauty who was protecting her fulsome breasts from the curious gaze of succeeding generations with a pair of feather dusters.

'Thank you, Felix, for those kind and optimistic words of hope and reassurance. I shall remember to pass your best wishes on to Lord Haw Haw,' said Tappy.

'Are you at all concerned about it, Tappy dear,' asked Arabella.

'Well, as I just mentioned, not been feeling quite the ticket lately and earlier today found out why. The results of the Arsocam arrived this morning and the upshot, if you would forgive the pun, is a long and complicated op on my capacious undercarriage. Yes, I know, where do the sawbones start? I'm not frightened, just bloody terrified. Far too young to leave the current Mrs Fawceytt and our sproglet Pongo Fawceytt the Third behind in this vale of tears. I mean, who will be doing all the complaining about the world and it's aunt if not yours truly? Can't help but feel that this is my El Alamein. It's shit or bust, excuse the pun again, with that sly old fox Rommel and the entire Afrika Korps waiting for me over the next sand dune. Still, I have you, my company of Desert Rats by my side and what a better bunch of chaps and chapesses to go into the fray with than you hard-bitten gang of warmongers.'

'Worrying news, Tappy darling. Chins up!'

'KBO old thing.'

'KBO!'

'You'll be fine Fawceytt Minor you malingering old dog.'

'Anyway. Enough of this Marjorie Proops stuff,' said Tappy. 'Are trumps still tits or shall we give diamonds a go?'

***

At the end of the evening Arabella wheeled Tappy into the garden where they sat in the mid-summer's fading light. Birdsong was in the air, all of the customers had gone home and Pippa had already said her goodnights and gone to bed. They shared a cigarette and conversed in conspiratorial whispers like a couple of teenagers, not wanting to disturb the hush.

'You don't seem your old self, Tappy, old thing,' said Arabella. 'Bit on edge aren't we. Want to share it with Mother?'

'I don't know what my old self is any more.'

'Your ill health is making you feel down, Tappy, darling, but the Winston Tappy I know and love will rise above it eventually. I will bring Snoots round for Schmackos, champers and cuddles with Pongo Fawceytt. And do Keep Buggering On, you poor thing.'

'You know what, Arabella. Back in the 1930s my salad days were a wonderful time. In the school holidays my life was simple and glorious. My donkey, Dandruff and I would travel for miles around the locality. The village shop had choco bars at thruppence a throw. There were 240 pennies to the pound, so choco heaven and the nascent stirrings of my capacious girth. Into the pub for a glass of lemonade and a bag of cripps in the garden. Smiths with a separate salt packet in a blue twist were a particular favourite. I addressed everyone I met as either "Mr" or "Mrs" or "Sir" or "Madam" — that's what everyone did! I did get several clips round the ear from the local plod — and quite right too. Beans were made by Heinz and nobody else and were full of tasty sugar and salt. Bacon was either smoked or streaky and sliced in Bixby's shop.

Butter came directly from the tub and was slapped into shape and wrapped in greaseproof paper. Beef dripping, spread thickly on home-baked bread and sprinkled with salt and pepper was the perfect supper. There was no idiot's lantern. Well, there was but nobody had one because there weren't any programmes, the radio was king. There was no alternative to the Home Service or The Light Programme and no PC or elf and safety — we didn't need it — people respected each other —'

Arabella gripped his hand and put a finger to her lips.

'What is it that is *really* bothering you, Tappy? What are all these endless rants about the "good old days" *really* about?'

Tappy stared into the darkening space of the summer garden as if the answer was just out of sight in the gathering gloom.

'Change, Arabella. I'm terrified of change.'

Arabella leant forward and touched his bruised-apple cheek.

'Everyone's terrified of change, Tappy, and that's because if you've seen enough change it means the end. Of everything. Of your world, of my world. Everything. You can never escape fear, Tappy. It's tangled up in life, whether you're climbing a mountain or just crossing the road. All you can do is embrace it.' She got up to go. 'Keep raging against the dying of the light, old friend.'

'What is this glue that binds us Arabella?' asked Tappy. 'You and I have always understood each other.'

'Evo Stik?' asked Arabella. She started down the path.

'Don't leave me Arabella. One more for the road? *In memorium* of dearest old Buggles? You didn't mind him, did you?'

'No, he was fine. A bit of a pain but a good friend.'

'Good night, Arabella,' he called after her, gently. 'See you next week, I hope?' He raised a hand to his fez in salute.

'See you next week,' said Arabella. 'And Keep Buggering On, Tappy love. It's all one can ever do.'

Tappy lingered alone in the garden as night lay its healing hand upon the world.

'You alright there, Tappy?' whispered a voice from the darkness.

'Who's that?'

'It's Danny Hucklesby.'

'Huckles, dear boy. It's nearly bloody midnight. I was just off to bed. What do you want?'

'I just wondered if you were having a lock-in.'

'I wasn't but I could do with some company. The Light of My Life has just retired and Arabella has also gone to the Land of Nod so I am alone with my thoughts and mired in my solitary despair.'

'Is that a yes?'

'Just one. Go and pour yourself a pint and fetch me a nightcap. Brandy Alexander please.'

'Yah what?' said Danny.

'I left the money on the bar,' said Danny on his return.

'To your good health,' said Tappy. 'And I mean that most sincerely, dear boy.' They clinked glasses.

'You okay?' said Danny. 'You seem a bit down.'

'Sound as a pound,' said Tappy unconvincingly. 'Sound as a bloody pound.'

A nightingale sang in Sickletree's Market Square.

'I've always loved this pub,' said Danny. 'It was the first place I visited when I came up here all those years ago — The Wonky Donkey. You were behind the bar and I bought a packet of pork scratchings and a lemonade for my nephew. Only he wasn't my nephew then. Just an obnoxious little shit.'

'I remember him. He looked like a little monkey. Quite rude.'

'That's him.'

'What happened to him?'

'They moved to America years ago. He's turned out fine, believe it or not. He's some sort of lawyer now.'

'The lucky little sod. I can't move to the water closet without somebody having the grace and goodwill to push me.'

'Can't get out of your chair at all?'

'Nope. Don't want to. It's safer in here. I hate everything about this bloody world and the least I engage with it the better.'

'I've been to those places in my life, Tappy, but it can get better. You wouldn't believe the number of times I've felt like that myself.'

'And what was your *modus operandi* in dealing with this curse of lack of motivation and the enveloping despair that is its bastard half-brother?'

'I would say the love of my family, which it is but it goes much deeper than that. It's also love of myself. I always thought that made you a narcissist but my mum-in-law taught me that way of thinking was wrong.'

'Old Mrs Yeo? What did she tell you.'

'Nothing. She *showed* me instead. Seven kids and all those grandkids and she never favoured or wavered in her love for them all. Oh, she could be a fierce old bugger alright and wouldn't hold back if she wanted to lay into you about something or other but she had this amazing respect for herself that always helped her do the right thing. She was a very wise woman, God bless her. And she stayed strong right up until the bitter end. She ended up in a wheelchair as well, remember?'

'Well, that's fine for Mrs Yeo and her enormous brood but it may have escaped your notice that the Light of My Life and my good self have no progeny excepting Pongo Fawceytt the Third of that lineage who can hardly be considered a blood relative.'

'Why do you always do that?'

'Do what?'

'Dream up a reason to excuse yourself for taking responsibility for your life and then dress it up in your pompous, public school waffle. I'm sure they didn't teach you that in the army.' Tough love. Another of Mrs Yeo's successful therapies.

'Hold hard there, Dr Sigmund Huckles, *mein freund*. This lock-in can be curtailed at any time you know. One reigns supreme in one's own back yard, in case you hadn't noticed and the patient's well-being is of primary importance.'

'You are much loved, Tappy. Consider every person that you meet as your family and friend and that problem is solved isn't it? We're all related underneath it all anyway, aren't we? The family of man and all that?'

'Goodness gracious Huckles. You will henceforth be known as Sigmund,' said Tappy and his bruised-apple face broke into a long overdue smile. 'One never understood that you are an amateur philosopher *and* shrink rolled up into one. Remind me to seek you out for another little chat when one feels the need for further psychiatric analysis. In the meantime you can bugger off back home. This couch is extremely uncomfortable and the session is over.' They clinked glasses one final time.

Danny walked up the path and turned to wave goodnight to Tappy. He watched from the darkness of an overhanging horse chestnut tree as the old soldier, thinking him gone, rose unsteadily from his wheelchair and hobbled slowly back into the pub.

Bedeman

I HAD BEEN INTRIGUED by the stately building that peeked through the oak trees on top of the hill since I was a young kid and the fascination only grew stronger with the passing years. The orange red brickwork glowed magically in the evening sun from the top of a Southern Vectis bus, solitary, serene and best of all, mysterious. Plenty there to capture the imagination of a young boy with time on his hands and the urge to explore. Over the years I developed the freedom and courage to roam the woods, beaches and fields that made up the monastery grounds just outside of Ryde on the Newport Road but the abbey itself continued to remain a secret and forbidding place to a lad without much confidence or any religious inclination. If our little gang of pirates ever did chance upon any of the monks on our explorations and adventures there was seldom any engagement other than a brisk nod or hello, which only added to the mystique of the place and its inhabitants.

So, it was with more than a little unease that I first walked through the gates of Quarr Abbey in the autumn of 1968 as a seventeen year-old student looking for an opportunity to study pottery as part of my foundation year at Portsmouth College of Art and Design. The first man I asked for help was a slight red-haired figure with a tightly cropped orange beard who looked the spitting image of Vincent van Gogh but with the exception that he possessed the regulation number of ears. By coincidence Father Bede Dunn was the monastery's potter and he welcomed the chance to pass on his knowledge, if not his abundant talent, to his callow apprentice. This began a friendship that lasted until his death in Australia in 2008. Over those years Father Bede, or Bedeman as he preferred to be called by his friends, had many adventures, not at all what you would expect from a man who had vowed to live a reclusive life. He was a lovely man but unsuited to his vocation — he could be a rogue, self-centred, egotistical, vain and self-opinionated — no saint but great fun, kind and, above all, someone who understood the human condition. We are born, we love, we live and we die. Nothing more than that, except the only reason we are here is (as he was so fond of repeating) that "God loves us to bits" and wants us to have a good time.

Bedeman was happy to help with the pottery and welcomed me with open arms into his workspace in the monastery cellars. I was allowed to live at Quarr during my internship there and eat and talk with the monks. During that time I got to know the people inside the habits and their personalities and their ways. I don't remember meeting anyone who could be considered a saint but I did meet some very nice people who were happy to share in their unusual and interesting lives. In the process I produced, thanks to Bedeman's steady hand, a half-decent tea set which unfortunately has been lost in the mists of time. But I do still have a plate with the Lion of Quarr stamp on the back and a drinking mug with my name on it, both the work of Bedeman.

To say Bedeman was unconventional is being kind. In truth he had a compulsively wild streak. It could have been the red hair or the excess alcohol but what was an undeniable fact was that he approached his life head on without reproach or regret. He liked a smoke and he liked a drink (and a few other forbidden pleasures on the side which are best left unrelated). On several occasions I was more than shocked by his frankness, outspoken opinions and inexplicable actions but we had some great adventures along with another friend who, together with Bedeman and myself, formed an Unholy Trinity of excess. This alliance eventually got us all into deep trouble, Bedeman was reprimanded for his shortcomings and my friend and I were banned from the monastery *sine die*. But those stories, if they are ever to be told, will be for another time.

Bedeman left Quarr soon after and worked in potteries in Holland and Australia and we lost touch for a long time. Many years after our earlier adventures I got a call whilst visiting the Isle of Wight. I recognised those plummy tones instantly.

Bedeman told me he was living back at Quarr and demanded we meet up to talk about old times and some new ones as well. Of course Bedeman being Bedeman he couldn't stay in one place for long (not a good trait for a monk) and he left for Australia once more where he started Peace Through Grieving — "A multi-faith funeral service to help and support anyone, of any culture, faith, religion, (or no religion) through the process of bereavement and to offer meaningful funeral or cremation services for the peace of mind and wishes of those closest to the deceased".

Despite being so far away and involved in such demanding work, Bedeman remianed in contact on a regular basis and our reacquaintance lasted until his death.

I had never been religious and was mystified by what power drove the monks to live what, to me, were such unusual and unnecessarily difficult, harsh and abstemious lives. But my short time spent living at Quarr on the pottery course all those years ago gave me an appreciation of monastic life and a basic understanding of how it was structured. The monks lived their days within a brutally inflexible order but also one of beauty and tranquility as well. And it was my basic knowledge of this simple structure that helped me to mirror the phases of a life within the Canonical Hours and use it as the inspiration and framework for *The Sickletree Hours* — a book of eight short stories which are fictional depictions of actual people and events. Autofiction, I believe it's called.

So, wherever you are dear old Bedeman, thank you for the adventures, the friendship and the tea set. You were an interesting and loyal friend and given the bizarre perfection of this life, it would not surprise me one bit if we were to bump into each other again. I know you'd probably hate this book but don't get your habit in a twist that I have written this little eulogy about you. After all, you said it yourself — "God loves us to bits and forgives us for everything". Which, for most of us, is probably just as well.

In loving memory of Father Bede Dunn
Paul Dibbens, February 2022

About the author

Paul Dibbens was born in Ryde on the Isle of Wight in 1951. He (sometimes) attended Sandown Grammar School in the 1960s and then studied at Portsmouth College of Art and Design from 1968 to 1972 before starting work as a graphic designer in London.

He has lived in Warwickshire since 1976 and is the head of Mustard Design, an award-winning graphic design company which serves as his creative outlet for a variety of projects. In continuous employment as a graphic designer for over fifty years, Paul still works part-time in his business and utilises his spare time by writing for enjoyment.

As part of his design work Paul has been involved in creating headlines, straplines and theme copy for ad campaigns and corporate literature. The brevity of expression and imagination necessary for success in this sphere has helped him to develop a vivid and colourful style which is perfect for creative writing.

Other books by Paul include *Grumblesea Goes Pop!* and *The Cockswine* which will both be available from Amazon in 2023.

Thank you!

With love and thanks to Editor, Sonia Baker, for all of the semi-colons, patience and her matchless sweet cucumber pickle. Also thanks to Ali D for her additional editorial input and Luke D for his proof reading and invaluable positivity, help and expertise in so many areas. Appreciation goes to friends Glenn Rogers and Neil McBrearty for taking the time to read the manuscript and offer their comments and Mike Jolliffe for the words of his song on the inside front cover. Finally, last but not least, I am indebted to long-time friend, colleague and fellow Sickletrean, Tim Porter, for his help in giving so much of his precious time to enliven this book with his wonderful series of illustrations.

This book was written for all of the people I've met on this long journey called life and I thank you for the love, help, advice, friendship and humour. Too many of you to mention here of course but you are in my heart and mind nonetheless and whether remembered or forgotten, the recipients of a heartfelt appreciation of the time and experiences we shared together.

Grumblesea Goes Pop!

Grumblesea Goes Pop! by Paul Dibbens is a saucy, sixties, seaside postcard of a book, that is filled with vivid imagery and colourful characters. It's a medley of farcical romp and coming of age drama that highlights the complexities of a youthful understanding of a troubling world and the ethical dualities of the times. Love and hate, peace and destruction, wisdom and stupidity, fun and despair are all present and depict the highs and lows of the human condition. Billy Sill, his family and friends, enemies and rock gods are caught up in the middle of it all, whilst the young man struggles to make sense of this most paradoxical and turbulent of times.

To follow is the first chapter of the book which is available from Amazon in 2023.

'My experience has been that life is an intricate blend of the ludicrous and profound which often gets taken to extremes. This book is my reflection on that observation and a love letter to "Grumblesea" as it was and hopefully still is.'

A DECISION MADE

"A Well Respected Man"
The Kinks (1965)

IN AN EXTRAVAGANT and gloriously oversized function room on the top floor of Grumblesea's town hall, Henry Louis Addie, two hundred and thirty-seventh mayor of the town and proprietor of the Three Whelks Café, was chairing an extraordinary general meeting of the Town Council. He sat pompously at the head of a gleaming table on a vintage velvet cushion which wasn't fulfilling its purpose of protecting him from the acute discomfort of a large cluster of only-just-bearable haemorrhoids. Needless to say, the incessant pain and irritation was making him even more petulant, short-tempered and spiteful than usual. Through the windows and above a dirty grey-green sea, menacing thunderheads were forming as a late winter storm gathered strength before deciding where to make landfall.

Mayor Addie was a tall, somewhat cadaverous man with a shock of effeminately styled, curly-grey bouffant hair who wore his heavy tortoiseshell spectacles precariously perched below a heavy brow. A violently receding, almost non-existent chin disappeared into the baggy neck of his stiffly starched shirt collar. As he spoke he continuously fidgeted irritably in his seat and nervously licked his thin lips with a snake-like rapidity. Rattling his official papers in vexation, he kicked out viciously at the manky and spoilt official Council Cat, Chairman Miaow, who was skulking under the table and taking a deepening interest with a razor-like claw in Addie's left sock garter. The cat ran like the devil it was, sinuously squeezed through the narrowly-opened door and emitted a shriek chilling enough to freeze the blood of heroes as it left the meeting for good.

The Executive Group of the Town Council had been urgently summoned to discuss one thing and one thing only — the expected and feared invasion of the "Great Unwashed", as Addie called them, at the proposed Grumblesea Pop Festival. Driven to distraction by the torment of his piles and a monstrous carbuncle on his foot Mayor Addie was now spitting nails. And, as if these ailments weren't bad enough, he had recently developed an irritating sniffle which, with the scarcity of time allotted for the meeting, meant he was having to clear his clogged nostrils without resorting to a hankie. It just about worked from his perspective but for the rest of the members of the Council it was maddening and, as a result, the meeting was becoming ever more fractious and divided.

The Mayor considered himself a man not to be reckoned with. He knew from genealogical research that he came from pirate stock, an ancestry which he felt gave him determination and a ruthless streak in times when lesser mortals wavered. His estimable ancestor had been the infamous Lop-eared Lou Addie, a privateer who had lost an ear on the Spanish Main to a careless cutlass swipe from a shipmate. Despite this handicap the pirate had, later in his career, become the eighteenth-century equivalent of a pools winner by liberating a home-bound Spanish galleon from its spectacular horde of treasure off the coast of Honduras.

Notoriously mean, subsequent generations of Addies had inherited their ancestor's wealth as well as his shrewdness in fiscal matters and through a portfolio of astute investments and a policy of never paying bills or buying rounds, the dynasty had steadily accrued a small fortune. This financial independence allowed Addie to indulge in his long-held ambition of becoming Town Mayor and lording it over his fellow citizens.

Unfortunately for him at this moment, Sidney Lilywhite, the Town Council's Treasurer, had hijacked the agenda and was pedantically and methodically going through the Council's yearly accounts with a fine tooth comb. It was a comb with just enough teeth missing to allow the nits of his financial impropriety to remain hidden and render him blameless for any missing sums of money. The ancient ship's bell that hung from the ornate ceiling had been rung three times and the meeting had begun. Officially, now that the procedure of civic government was in motion, convention stated that there should be no interruptions to the process until the bell was once again rung three times to signify the end of the meeting proper and the start of any other business.

As well as Lilywhite's shady manoeuvring with the Council's finances, what was also expertly concealed was the fact that he was regularly filching not inconsequential sums of cash from the Bowls Club on his twice-monthly bar nights. "Two for you and one for me", was his oft-repeated mantra as the till ka-chinged. In those mainly straight-laced times it would have shocked his fellow committee members to know that, beneath his immaculate blazer, Council tie and neatly pressed slacks, the official had decided not to wear any underwear. Universally mistrusted, nothing was ever quite what it seemed with Treasurer Lilywhite.

'Water, Gas and Electricity,' he uttered in a sinister West Country burr. 'Four pounds, two shillings and sixpence, ha'penny.'

He twiddled his spiv-like moustache and flattened what would normally be a slicked-back widow's peak hairstyle but which now bore the remnants of the huge blob of gull droppings which had landed on his head on the way to the meeting. Why, oh why, hadn't he taken the wife's advice and worn a hat? It now looked as if he was sporting an overgrown peroxided crew cut.

The other councillors muttered, sighed, groaned and fidgeted in boredom while a grandfather clock, embellished with sailing ships foundering in wildly exaggerated tempests and with the legend "Here be Dragons" on its face, ticked monotonously in time with Lilywhite's monologue. Mayor Addie looked impatiently at his watch as a sudden squall of sleet mixed with heavy rain hammered on the windows as if impatient to be let in. The gust of frigid air breeched the decaying frames and forced the heavy festoon curtains to billow outwards and release a cloud of moths.

'Yes, yes, yes —' said Addie interjecting irritably, 'but we will have to curtail the Treasurer's oration at this juncture for more — *hmph* — pressing matters. Let us first take a refreshment break and then we must get on to item fourteen.' He cleared his throat emphatically. 'Apropos the proposed Grumblesea Pop Festival.'

Lilywhite, his balloon of self-importance pricked, stumbled to an abject halt mid-sentence whilst others around the table indulged in a mumbled chorus of approval. A scraping of chairs on the wooden floorboards followed Addie's diktat as the committee formally rose as one and hastily adjourned to the end of the room where a tray of tepid tea and stale fairy cakes was waiting.

The room in which the Council members were gathered reflected the false grandeur and duplicity of the members themselves and to conduct a sprightly circuit of the damp, fungus-mottled, yellowing walls of the chamber was a painful lesson in the dreariness and hubris of civic pride. These dry-as-dust tours were often retributive and enacted on unwilling bigwigs from other equally unimpressive towns and cities as a form of punishment for having inflicted similar ordeals on Grumblesea dignitaries in the past.

Hung on the west wall were two huge and beautifully engraved Georgian maps which, though typographically masterful, were in fact topographically hopelessly inaccurate. These vintage and painstakingly crafted hand-coloured surveys were extremely fanciful depictions of the fishing villages of Upper and Lower Grumble, bisected by the then picturesque but now foetid Grumble Brook. Captured well before the villages were merged into the town of Grumblesea and created with the confidence of burgeoning empire, they bore the emblem of the celebrated map-makers Felcher & Fackwitt of London. On the north wall was draped a huge, sea-stained white ensign, wind-tattered on its lee edge and rescued from the wreck of *HMS Obnoxious* which had foundered on Grumble Sands in 1709. Arrayed on the east wall was a selection of portraits of previous mayors of Grumblesea, chosen by the status and prestige of the sitter rather than any artistic merit of the painter or comeliness of the subject. Consequently, the row of images, united only in a shared quality of hideousness and menace, glared down on the observer like a down-the-ages identity parade for a particularly ugly and vicious, but thankfully, long-forgotten crime. Skirting the south wall and facing the sea below a line of rain-spattered windows was a miscellany of immaculately polished trophy cabinets. Fashioned in walnut, teak and mahogany, they held a multiplicity of trophies and ornaments which, in the main, were totally irrelevant to the town itself: it was as if someone had toured all the jumble sales in the wider area, collected whatever irrelevant tat they could find and thrown it arbitrarily into the display cases.

Amongst the dubious awards was a trophy for the winner of a darts competition in the village of Tittwell, located at least one hundred miles from the Grumblesea area, and a flower arranging cup that had been clumsily engraved with the simple inscription "Avis Heckles. Green-finger Girl. Piddley Regis W.I. 1924". The only trophy with even a shadow of merit or relevance was a huge shield that took centre stage in the largest cabinet in the display. Centrally placed and subtly lit by an array of flyspecked spotlights, it boasted the legend "Southern England's Cleanest Seaside Town" and was bedecked with ribbons in the town colours of orange and blue. However, what was not known outside of immediate Council circles, was that even this supposed triumph was tainted by deception. The Town Council had been tipped off as to when the supposedly anonymous judges would be visiting and there had just been enough time for a panicked and hastily arranged clean up of the chip-paper strewn and seagull-crap splattered seafront to be implemented. This tip-off was facilitated with a bribe in the form of a free slap-up meal at Addie's Three Whelks Café, where the grandees unknowingly gambled with the possibility of contracting botulism with every mouthful they ate. This enticement had been further enhanced by the added inducement of twenty pounds per judge, embezzled from the Council funds by the sleight of Treasurer Lilywhite's pen. The bribe took the form of four moth-eaten fivers, concealed in a brown paper envelope and stuffed furtively into relevant back pockets by the Mayor himself as he waited at table during the meal. Erroneously, each envelope was adorned with the town crest and bore the Council's motto "Honesty, integrity and fairness in all our doings".

'As you know the organisers are proposing a huge event for at least one hundred and fifty thousand people,' resumed Addie after the indigestible refreshments had been dispatched. 'These, I hesitate to call them people, will be sleeping in the open — *hmph* — without the provision of even the most basic sanitation and we need to be in possession of powers to enforce regulations in order to avoid an epidemic that could affect the health of every resident of our town — *hmph!*' Addie had unveiled so many monuments and opened so many civic buildings in his time he just didn't know when to stop. His pomposity engine was in overdrive, his nose, carbuncle and piles now worse than ever — he had to be interrupted, and he was.

'Yes, yes, yes!' interjected an equally choleric Albert Tosser of Nineveh Farm which was located on the outskirts of town and boasted the perfect site for the proposed festival. His nascent comb-over flapped sideways as he spun his head about while looking around the table.

'Let's cut all the crap, for Christ's sake and just make a decision this time. This has been going on for months. As you know I'm well up for it as this town desperately needs a kick up the arse and some serious investment. It's still stuck in the nineteenth bloody century.' As an elected officer of an organisation supposedly dedicated to the welfare and service of others, this member of the Council could be remarkably self-serving.

Tosser clenched his huge ham-like fists in frustration and pounded them on the table in order to emphasise his words. A crippling financial situation brought about by a failed holiday homes venture and an out-of-control gambling addiction had made him desperate to get the festival up and running and the payment for hiring out his land for only a few days would resolve all of his money worries in one fell swoop.

This was too much for Vice-Admiral Mostyn Peasebody, highly decorated sailor and self-appointed protector of the town's morals and outdated Victorian ideals. His plummy public school pronunciation and elevated rank betrayed his social standing: no career cul-de-sac at Chief Petty Officer for him.

'Yes, and we all know why that is don't we? It has nothing to do with benefiting the town, demm you and everything to do with you *rentin'* your land to these slimy pop creatures and *linin'* your grubby pockets with the proceeds as a result. Now, we at the Fishwick Defence League are against —'

'Everything. You're against everything, you bloody old stuffed shirt,' exploded Tosser. 'You puffed up bag of wind, you —' He was in full "Get *on* not *off* my land" mode.

His tirade tailed away as he in turn was interrupted by a large, copiously-bosomed woman of about fifty who was crammed into a semi-transparent chiffon dress. Her outfit acted much like the skin of a sausage: pulled as tight as it could be, it gave an unfettered view of several semi-intimate nooks and crannies which probably should have remained hidden.

'Gentleman, gentleman, *please* —' she simpered. 'If I may have my say. I personally think that financially, culturally and in PR terms the festival would be truly excellent for the town. To be elevated to the international stage by such a high profile event is a once-in-a-lifetime opportunity for our community and definitely not to be sniffed at. I can't put it strongly enough. *We need to market the town.*'

'It's already *got* a blitherin' market. It's on Satdees in Petticoat Way,' said Peasebody irritably. 'The memsahib bought me a pair of brown socks there only last week and the barrow boy chappie threw in some garters for free,' he added helpfully.

Super-sized earth mother Dolores Putfarker was a lady with an altruistic and compassionate nature who had recently used an empty life to motivate herself into starting a late career as a portrait painter. Unfortunately, so bad was her work that most of her unveiling sessions were punctuated by the exclamation "Who is it?" as each of her artistic endeavours usually involved some form of physical deformity which rendered the artwork unrecognisable to close friends, relatives and, often, even the sitter themselves.

Grumblesea, with its wonderful light and proximity to the sea had been the ideal place to have her studio and Putfarker Portraiture had rapidly acquired a laughable reputation amongst the Grumblesea artistic *cognoscenti* for the quality of her work. Nevertheless, she'd persevered in her desperate attempts to ingratiate herself with the higher orders of the municipality by attaining a seat on the Town Council and working hard for the betterment of the little town and its apathetic townsfolk. But why was a woman of independent means and with a career in the creative arts so desperate to serve the community? The answer lay in a sordid episode in her recent past.

What had then seemed such a beautiful and natural idea had since driven her to the depths of despair and degradation and the disgust of her fellow Grumbleseans. The truth was, Putfarker was a fallen woman.

She had attended a garden party held for the Arts Society at the vicarage in the Summer of Love. The Reverend Basil Whiffler, twenty-three years her senior, had shown an interest in her work, the communion wine had flowed like water and one thing had led to another. Before she even knew it, His Reverence was administering "extreme unction" to her over the font in the nave of his church while through the medieval glass windows the afternoon sunlight artfully dappled her dimpled bottom with flickering coloured rays. Unfortunately, the lovers were discovered *in flagrante delicto* by a horrified teenager who had arrived early for choir practice and who subsequently cheerily informed the Bishop that his church was being used as a "knocking shop". Whiffler was temporarily

Dolores Putfarker.
'Who is it?'

defrocked and packed off to a mission in Madagascar where he continued his carousing with the native population and Putfarker was left to mourn the only true love of her life and carry a guilt which in turn inspired a fanatic's obsession to atone for her sin.

Embarrassingly for Putfarker, sitting opposite her at the table was the Reverend Whiffler himself, just back from exile and also keen to atone for his *erreur des amoureux* in the eyes of the townsfolk, but sexually frustrated nonetheless. Since the affair had become known to her, Mrs Whiffler had withdrawn completely from her duties in the coitus department and, what with there being a dearth of compliant Madagascan girls in Grumblesea, Whiffler had become increasingly desperate. Unfortunately, old habits die hard and the over-sexed cleric had confidently but mistakenly been playing footsie throughout the meeting with a confused and alarmed Treasurer Lilywhite who was seated next to Putfarker and becoming unwillingly drawn into a potential *ménage à trois*.

'I agree with Dolores,' said Whiffler. His compliance was nothing more than a sly bid to resume extra-marital activities with the large lady sitting opposite him.

'Well, you would, wouldn't you,' muttered Addie. He didn't know it but he was deeply jealous of the vicar as Mrs Addie had long preceded Mrs Whiffler in taking a negative attitude towards the pleasures of the flesh.

'Come on, everyone. Such cynicism from some quarters. This is a great little town and we need to show it off. It's a marvellous place for wildlife for instance — there are red squirrels here and talk of reintroducing sea eagles. We even get porpoises and seals in the seas off our beaches,' gushed Putfarker.

'And jellyfish and sharks,' offered a sulky Lilywhite.

'And manta rays,' lied Peasebody.

'Complete and utter rubbish,' said Tosser. 'They're tope.

Hardly great whites are they? Tope are just little bloody tiddlers. The best they can do is give you a nasty suck.'

'Have you ever been face-to-face with a Portuguese man o' war?' asked Peasebody angrily. ''Cos I demm well have. Back in forty-five it was. I was doin' a bit of snorklin' off Gilkicker Point, just back from Malta I was, and the blighter came at me with his tentacles spread like —'

'Sorry to interrupt, but I'll say it again. Grumblesea is a marvellous place but it is in decline and has been for years,' said Putfarker. 'And the attitude of some on this Council seems to be that they want it to stay that way forever and a day.'

'If it's such a marvellous place, all the more reason not to bugger it up then,' said Lilywhite. 'Which brings me on to the important matter of the extravagant annual expenditure on the maintenance of the town's public parks and gardens —'

'He had enormous teeth like *blitherin'* razors and a sting like a cattle prod,' persisted Peasebody.

'Who?' chorused everyone.

'The Portuguese jelly thing of course. Pay attention on the lower deck, that rating.'

'Oh, give it a rest. You lot make me sick with your mealy-mouthed platitudes. Progress frightens the shit out of you lot doesn't it?' An increasingly desperate Tosser had sensed that the golden egg was beginning to slip from his grasp.

'There are so many things that we could do as an adjunct to the festival to increase our perceived standing in the community. A Battle of the Bands is just one idea. It could be for local groups and the winner could play a short set at the festival itself — I think that would go down really well with the media *and* the townsfolk,' said Putfarker.

'I think it's a disgrace,' said Peasebody. 'They'll be *bonkin'* in the churchyard, *bonkin'* under the hedges, *bonkin'* in the fields, *bonkin'* in the village bloody shop, *bonkin'* in the, er, um —' He momentarily ran out of locations in which to bonk.

'*Councillors!* The matter in hand if you please,' Addie banged his official oak gavel hard onto the table several times. The meeting had degenerated into the usual farce. 'We keep digressing. I repeat, the matter in hand if you please. This damned festival.'

'Quite right. As I'm sure Mayor Addie will agree, we need to take a vote and settle the matter irrevocably. As I have said many times before, I'm definitely an "aye".' Putfarker prematurely raised a hand the shape of a bag of sausages.

'Yes, we know,' murmured Addie vindictively to himself. 'You say "aye" to anything in trousers.'

'Drawing lots is what we need. Sort the swabs out once and for all and keelhaul the transgressors.' Peasebody's gimlet eyes scanned the room searching out mutineers. '*Give that rating thirty lashes of the cat*,' he shouted as his gaze fell on Whiffler.

Oh no, he's lost it again thought Addie. 'You can't do that any more Mostyn,' he said gently. 'The cat o' nine tails — it's forbidden. Quite some time ago actually.'

'I'll be demmed if I can't,' muttered Peasebody grumpily. 'You'd better not come aboard my ship.'

'Yes, thank you, Mostyn. This whole affair needs to be seen to be conducted in a squeaky clean and above board manner given recent — *hmph* — indiscretions from some members of the Council.' Addie couldn't stop himself from throwing a sly dig at Putfarker and Whiffler.

'All those in favour of the event taking place please raise — *hmph* — your right hand. Would the committee please note that Mr Tosser, Reverend Whiffler and Miss Putfarker are "ayes". There are three — *hmph* — "ayes",' he pompously proclaimed.

'Now, all those *against* the festival raise your right hand,' instructed Addie. He then raised his own arm, looked needlessly around the table with his nose in the air and counted.

'Please note for the record that — *hmph* — Vice-Admiral Peasebody, Treasurer Lilywhite and myself, the Lord Mayor, are "nays".' The councillors groaned unanimously.

'Usually in the event of a tie, I, as Chairman, would have the casting vote but, in this case and with a decision on such an important and fractious matter to take, I think it important for — *hmph* — PR reasons, to be seen to be squeaky clean, as it were.'

Addie was very nervous about how the decision would be greeted by the outside world and was obviously determined to absolve himself of any complicity in the outcome. In this instance, passing the buck would appear to be the sensible option.

'This is too much responsibility to place on one single man, even somebody as elevated as the Lord Mayor himself,' he suggested officiously. 'So I recommend we resolve it in the time-honoured way. The toss of a coin — *hmph* — *hmph* — *hmph!*'

The table murmured agreement. Anything to get the job done and then off to the pub. Putfarker briefly considered loaning Addie her rose-scented hankie.

'I would suggest — *hmph* — heads we go ahead, tails we do not? Excellent. Miss Putfarker? As the *lady* — ?' He emphasised the word "lady" with a slight but noticeable distaste, which made his opinions on her sordid affair with the vicar apparent one final time. 'If you would — *hmph* — be so kind — *hmph!*'

Addie handed Putfarker the Council's pristine George the Third gold sovereign at the same moment as having his final and most drastic nasal meltdown of the meeting. The coin had been donated to the town in the dim and distant past by the East India Company and had been reserved in perpetuity for such occasions.

As it passed across the table, Addie anointed it with a sneeze.

Putfarker flipped the coin and it span upwards into the oppressive atmosphere. You could have heard a pin drop as it completed its journey to and from a ceiling illustrated with a grandiloquent depiction of the Battle of Tompkin's Toe. The coin penetrated a transparent veil of ancient cobwebs and, cocooned in the gossamer fibre, returned into the clammy grasp of Putfarker's pudgy fingers. Slamming it down hard onto the polished veneer she looked around at the Council members, fixing each and every one in the eye with a meaningful look and thoroughly enjoying the power she was holding over the men.

'Heads we go ahead with the festival, tails we do not,' repeated Addie solemnly.

Putfarker slowly and dramatically removed her hand to reveal the coin. The head of poor Mad King George could just be seen through the ancient cobweb, peering up at Putfarker with a slightly triumphant and unbalanced smirk, as if out of the heavily frosted window of a lunatic asylum.